Otter Tracks

From the River to the Island

Ross Paul Lawford

ISBN: 9798690448455

For Daniel

"The fundamental love that a man needs in his life, if he is to have steady spiritual ease is the love of place where he was a child, and first became aware of the light, and the objects which the light illumined ... It is the hurt child become man that seeks the wilderness, wherein to rebuild himself."

(Henry Williamson)

CONTENTS

ACKNOWLEDGMENTS

Firstly, I'd like to say a huge thank you to Alison Norman for her brilliant editing skills and friendship, this couldn't have been done without you.

And to the talented Pam Doore for the time and effort of bringing the cover to life with her wonderful artwork.

Many thanks to Anne Williamson for giving extremely helpful advice and for allowing me to use a wonderful quote by Henry Williamson.

Thank you to the late Henry Williamson for writing "Tarka" and making me fall in love with Otters when I was young.

Thank you to Paul Yokon and everyone at the International Otter Survival Fund for the work you do for Otters globally.

Thank to Paul, Denise and the boys for being there at a time when I needed someone.

To Amy, your light will always shine.

To Mr Chris Griffin for the unrivalled adventures.

A big thank you to Chris James for giving me a chance on the Island.

Thank you to Alice Thomson for her help.

Another thanks to all the people I've met along the way that have greatly helped me on my journey.

A special thank you to the Princes Trust whose training programme was a big game changer for me and continues to be for many young people across the country.

The natural world is an incredible source of inspiration and guidance and although you can't hear this, I thank you whole heartedly.

Thanks to the little Otter Squeaks who changed the course of my journey.

Thank you to Vale Wildlife Rescue for giving me the chance I needed.

The biggest thank you to my Mom and Dad for their boundless patience and love.

A huge thanks to all my family.

A massive thank you to Kerry for inspiring me despite my relentless nature.

And lastly to Daniel for his pure, wild innocence.

Prologue

Coming Out of the Darkness

The first thing that comes to my mind on how to describe the way I felt before I met her was like a terrified lone Fox being hunted on horseback.

That's the first thing that comes to my mind when I stare down at the blank page beneath me - it's not a thought that lingers too long in my mind; it's a cliché of depression and anxiety. To be truthful, when I think about the trauma that engulfed me, it's almost too hard to reach that place. My mind over those two or three years is hazy to say the least, and as much as possible has been blocked out. I know the events and the suffocating feelings happened but putting it all down in some form of order would be sketchy. To draw on a Fox being chased and then, ultimately being caught, as a memory of my own depression, would suggest that before being chased, I was free in the first place. In my mind I was anything but - the fact that I was chased and caught during the hunt seems much more appropriate. Trapped, caged, held down, unable to escape, unsafe, confused, these are the words that enter my mind first when I stare again at the empty page.

I was my own worst enemy, and looking for someone to blame wouldn't be fair on anyone. If anything, I liked the protection that depression gave me, giving me the opportunity to hide away and complain to myself about how unfair my life was.

It was more like being trapped behind a translucent piece of ice; the light filters in but the shapes don't make any sense and it's hard to completely focus on them.

A few years previously I'd read Tarka the Otter; it's a beautiful but harrowing tale. I'd drift away and spend many hours with the little Otter as he journeyed across the Devonshire landscape. I felt an affinity with him. Most of his time was spent running, scared, unable to settle anywhere for long and that's something I could relate to. The dream of seeing a wild Otter was so far-fetched and unimaginable - just the thought of going outside was enough to send me into a massive panicky state.

Months went by with very little light filtering into my head. It could take me hours and sometimes days to get to the point of just thinking of going out. The wall I'd built up around me was enough to show those nearest me that I was alright - at least on the outside. I was lonely, and despite being close to my family, I was distant. I was always under attack from myself, constantly looking for the safest way to escape - it didn't matter where I was, I always felt threatened.

I felt a slight change the day I started staring of out my window and seeing birds flying over the house. I was distracted by watching other things move around from the relative safety of my room; they distracted me from my thoughts, inside my icy bubble.

I started watching a pair of Blue Tits flitting around the Holly bush in the front garden, they would nervously fly to the feeder, constantly checking in every direction for predators before retreating to the safety of the Holly bush. That fear of being out in the open space was something I could relate to as well. The House Sparrows that would sit on top of the Privet hedge looked at ease with their surroundings, they didn't look nervous or threatened - they were content in their territory, and it showed with their behaviour.

A lot of wild animals seem to spend a large amount of their time acting afraid and nervous, especially when away from their comfort zones. I started to notice that as the days went on, the Blue Tits became gradually less afraid. If they, in such a short amount of time, could adapt to a situation, then so could I.

On a cold wintry Monday in the middle of the day, I ventured out for the first time in a long while; it felt like the first time I'd ever been outside. I picked midday, at the start of the week, because I thought it would be the quietest time to avoid contact with the fewest people possible. I cycled to the cemetery which was less than a few minutes away - I could've walked it in five minutes but the bike was crucial, I needed the protection that I thought the bike would give me - the ability to escape.

The old cemetery was accessed by a small gate that led me underneath a section of mature Pine trees. I leant against one of the trunks, I felt like my heart was going to explode, my breathing was heavy and out of control. The journey to get here horrible, it only took a few minutes but, in that time, I was petrified, like there was a threat around me in all directions. I pushed my bike to a spot in the path where I could see in every direction; this would give me time to escape if anyone did approach. I knew deep down that my thoughts weren't rational, but, in that moment, they were a genuine threat.

After ten minutes, an old lady carrying a bunch of mainly white flowers wrapped in cellophane approached slowly from the far end. Just the sight of someone in this space made my hands shake. I retreated to the safety of an overgrown evergreen - I could see her from here. She headed gingerly to an old grey gravestone that was neatly mowed around the edges, in contrast to the surrounding area which was left to grow wild. Long grass covered the bases of most of the stones, some of which had been completely taken over by twisted Ivy and Bramble but were attempting to reclaim the many gravel paths. I watched as she unwrapped the covering and gently laid the flowers against the headstone. I fell to my knees and tucked myself in against the soft feel of the roots. Watching the lady from here felt like I wasn't even there at all, like I was watching it on a big screen, and nothing could hurt me. A Robin joins me underneath the thick evergreen, he flits around the floor, turning over pieces of the soft blanket of earth and composting needles. He picks a small worm and flies through the dark arches of the branches to feed on his find. I look back to find the elderly lady has been replaced by a Jay. The dirty pink bird stands alert at the top of the stone, he tilts his head to get a look at the newly placed flowers, he's carrying a bronze-coloured acorn in his beak. His head is a mix of cream and black streaks but it's hard to avoid his beady eyes that have finally noticed the crumpled shape sitting in the darkness. Six of the longest minutes of my life pass by in slow motion. The Jay adjusts his black feet on the stone before prancing around in a kind of display dance, although to my knowledge, it was just me observing him. I was desperate to get out from my comforting base under the tree, but I wasn't leaving until the entertaining bird in front of me had flown. He tapped the acorn against the stone and several strikes later the protective casing falls to the ground. Finally, he spreads his wings, the stunning flash of sparkly blue catches my eye, then grey meets black at the bottom of the wings as white patches fall off the blue flashes. The dirty pink bird pushes its wings down even faster before angling its body in between a row of Silver Birch and away.

The short trip home was nowhere near as tormenting as the one to get there, but I was still relieved to get back to the sanctuary of my room. I considered "operation get out the door" to be a successful one.

That was my first venture outside, and I had a couple more in the week that followed, but it's the only one I can remember clearly enough to describe. After that day I could feel the icy shield around me begin to melt.

A much longer venture came a few weeks later - I'd prepared for it like a secret army mission, with exact precision. I'd been planning it for days - the place, the time of day, the clothing, even the weather had to be just right. Thankfully, on this day it was.

Every second of the journey was terrifying. I've done this journey many times since and it only takes about twenty-five minutes, but it felt like an attack the whole way. The last section through the windy lane that led between a section of large white houses was when the fear closed in on me the most. I suddenly had horrible thoughts of being chased from behind and attacked from the sides.

Thankfully, I reached a gate that looked upon a field that was bare and devoid of life. In the distance I could see the familiar sight of the first school I went to and an Oak that I used to climb - reassurance that I'd been here before, and no harm came to me. I leant against the wooden gate and fought hard to get my breath back, my heart was once again trying to break out of my chest.

Finally, my breathing and heart rate fell back to a normal pace. I looked around the field for signs of life, but nothing showed except for the view of my childhood. It felt comforting to me.

The early spring wind rattled through the trees behind me and made an eerie whistling sound as it passed through leafless branches. I didn't flinch, I wasn't scared here.

I tentatively crept down the steep slope making sure I kept to the side that has the clearest view of what's around me. Nothing moved in the wood and there were no noises coming out, not even bird song. I knew the river lay at the bottom of the track, but it felt like an eternity to get there and there was no sight of it ahead. The path was beginning to feel like it was taking me somewhere I didn't want to go, it felt like a trap. I jumped off the track and skulked into the protection of the wood, the leaves of Wood Anemones and Primrose pierced the ground but were still waiting for the flowers to bloom. I twisted and bent under branches and stepped over fallen trees whilst trying successfully not to slide down the slope that was getting muddier with every step. As I pulled back a tangled mess of overgrown and dead Brambles, I could see the flow of the river. My excitement grew quickly and my fear all but disappeared.

On the edge of the river was an old, well-worn fallen Beech tree, the touch it of felt smooth and welcoming. The view across the river from here bled senses into me that I haven't felt for a long time. I'd sat on this tree before and watched a Kingfisher fishing in autumn. Today the leaves aren't out, and the trees are bare but it's still as beautiful as I remember it. I had to get here. For whatever reason, this is the place I could reconnect with what I knew.

Over the coming months, I found solace from the natural world and comfort from the animals living there. I spent many hours sitting on that fallen tree that sat through the woods at the edge of the river. I'd get lost within the beautiful surroundings, watching the seasons around me change. The river and the woods inevitably became my safe-haven and the only place I felt free, until I was ready to start again. I had wasted at least two years of my life that I would never get back again.

And then, in a relatively short space of time, I was going to go through an even bigger change ...

Squeaks

I was sat on the familiar fallen Beech tree with an opportunity racing around my head; I had the chance to join a course that could potentially get me back into the world for real - not hiding behind Brambles or old stone walls, but actually out in the open. After a long drawn out conversation with a particularly confiding Robin and an interrupting Blackbird I decided to go for it.

I was lucky enough to be able to join the course a week after its start date; the idea for the programme was to breathe new confidence and life skills into people just like me. Most of it was set outdoors which suited me - I could express myself in a different way.

One of the sections on the course, which was nearer the end of the twelve-week programme was a community project, I'd been looking forward to it from the start. It could be anything from mowing lawns and putting up new fences at a Care Home to renovating crumbling paths in town parks. Fortunately for me, a chance phone call to an Animal Sanctuary and their need for a new home for a female Otter changed everything. Fate, luck or just being in the right place at the right time? Whatever, it was it was the best thing that could've happened to me.

I went to the Centre and began work on the site, which was muddy, flat and empty of anything except an old Apple tree. I, with the help of others, set upon digging out a stream that would lead to a pond at the bottom and used the soil to make a mound at the top. It took us a week to complete the new home for the Otter who was being kept out of sight at the back of the Sanctuary. When we were done, it had a flowing stream, a new artificial holt, new turf and a wooden bridge that crossed the stream. On the few occasions that I had headed up to see the Otter whom we'd built a home for, she'd been sleeping every time.

The owners had promised me free visits to the Sanctuary, so I took full advantage of this gift. On my first visit back to the Animal Sanctuary since helping build the enclosure for the Otter, which, incidentally, I was yet to see finished, was even more glorious than the time I spent there whilst on the project.

I wandered around from the Aviaries at the bottom to the open Deer field at the top. A Snowy Owl sat majestically across from the menacing Wildcats. The Reptile House was filled with wonderful and exotic creatures from large Pythons and intimidating looking Tarantulas, to the prehistoric looking Iguanas. Fruit Bats slept upside down under red lights as Rodents scurried and scratched in the opposite enclosures. A small army of Meerkats stood on guard in their sandy home whilst the cheeky Raccoons slept through until dusk.

I reached an enclosure which sat behind a wild and overgrown area where rescued Foxes lurked behind the nettles. Next to them was the last enclosure on this section and the one I wanted to see the most, as well as its new resident. This is the enclosure I helped to build, and I couldn't wait to see the stream flow and, hopefully, the elusive Otter. I peered over the wooden sloped fence to see the animal living within.

There was a stream running down a bank that led into a small pool at the bottom. A large felted box sat under an Apple tree but there was no sign of any animal. I waited patiently on the sloped fence with a couple of pieces of clear Perspex to view through. Ten minutes went by with no more than a pair of Blue Tits in the Apple tree and a passing Red Admiral butterfly to observe. Then, movement by the box, the little Otter bounds out, armed with an abundance of energy; she's like a coiled spring that's been released. She stands on her back legs to get that little bit taller to best view the man staring straight back. Her deep hazel eyes stare me down as her nose twitches uncontrollably whilst her long whiskers drape down to cover her pale cheeks, her front paws grasped together as she let out a quiet squeak - which is why she was given the name, Squeaks. She was amazing.

There was a vulnerability in her eyes, inquisitively asking questions of me and squeaking out loudly every time I ducked my head down to hide, then popped back up. Other visitors would come and see her, stay for a few minutes then move on once she'd posed for a photo. I remained and was captivated by her every move.

Every chance I had, I made the journey over to see her, just to observe what she was up to, which for most of the time was sleeping in her oversized box. She was like a new toy that made me feel more alive than anything I'd ever encountered before.

Every now and then she would peek out of her box sensing somebody there, joyfully bouncing over, peeping and squeaking as she came.

I looked at the staff around me and thought this must be the absolute dream, to spend every day with these animals and get paid for the privilege. I couldn't think of a better way to spend my day, going into enclosures and mucking out, talking to visitors and seemingly sounding knowledgeable about my subject.

I began volunteering at the Sanctuary to get even closer to her. I devoted as much time as I possibly could as it was the only place I wanted to be; I felt safe in that bubble away from the outside world. I guess it was the opposite feeling for most of the animals, but for me, I'd found a place I was accepted; the animals, especially, Squeaks, didn't judge me or ask too much of me.

As much attention as I showed her, she started demanding more and more of mine. I'd be cleaning out the Aviaries or grooming the horses and I'd hear her calling across the Sanctuary. She would sometimes refuse to be quiet until I appeared. None of my old fears and anxiety showed themselves here and even places outside the Sanctuary didn't affect me nearly as much.

It was coming up to Christmas and I'd offered to come in on Christmas Eve as the Sanctuary was short on staff and helpers. I couldn't think of anywhere I'd rather be, spending the day with the animals, and, Squeaks, in particular. I'd got up earlier than usual and walked through the town towards the train station. I stared out of the window onto fields that were glimmering under the light from a full moon. A Fox sat still on an embankment in half-light as the train slowed before my stop. It was a beautiful crisp winter's day with barely any wind, the sun entered the sky just before reaching the top of the hill where the Centre sat, in the midst of an old Orchard. The ground around the main gate where rain usually congregated was frozen over, and, after a poor attempt at solo figure skating, I headed into the Sanctuary.

I opened all the gates and turned on the lights in the indoor areas. I passed on my seasonal greetings to all the animals along the way. Even the Stick Insects got a cheery Merry Christmas, although it was met with a static response. The Deer paddock glistened with a hardened frost as the low sun shone down. Everything was beautiful and, Squeaks, well, that little Otter was wonderful that day. Once all the other animals had been tended to, I went straight back to her and spent the remainder of the day with her. It was one of the first times she let me stroke her back and poke her nose without aggressively warning me off - a real breakthrough with an animal who was normally very wary of people. Over time she must've got used to the man watching her every subtle move and bringing her fresh fish. I didn't push her for attention, and she didn't beg me for it, it felt like a space we could both just breathe without being forced to conform. I saved the biggest Happy Christmas message and thank you for her.

Not long before leaving to join the usual festivities I was called into the makeshift office, and, after a brief phone conversation, I was offered a full-time staff position at the Sanctuary. I couldn't work out if this was an elaborate joke or dream; it turned out to be closer to the latter. I hold Squeaks completely responsible for this gift, and on Christmas Eve of all days. Without that chance phone call, we would never have met.

Over the next few months, I got closer and closer to her and she became a lot less timid around me. Maybe I gave her the attention she'd been craving, without pushing her to perform. I would sit in with her once everyone had gone, just sitting in her space letting her get used to me being around, getting accustomed to my smell and the way I moved. She would, at first, be a little aggressive towards me, but as time went on, she became much more relaxed by my presence, seemingly finding comfort in me as I did in her. When I approached her enclosure coming up the gravel path, I could hear Squeaks get louder and louder with an almost excited tone. When I peered over the ledge, she would be waiting for me with expectant eyes. I would drop her a fish and she'd grab it and run for her water pool to wash and swim with it before devouring her snack. In the wild her species is highly sociable and playful, but here, she was alone with a loneliness in her eyes that I hoped I helped take away, as she was helping to take away mine. I ended up living at the Sanctuary, just a stone's throw away from her enclosure. I got to spend even more time with her than I'd ever imagined.

The days were steadily getting colder with sharper frosts and the occasional winter storm. I started putting a lot more straw and an old comfy blanket of mine in her makeshift holt to keep her warm against the cold winter nights. One morning, at the end of January, I woke up to a hard frost that had managed to create ice crystal patterns on my window. I went outside and everything was white; the trees, the field, the path and all the wooden enclosures were covered in a frosty shield. I headed straight up the track towards her enclosure. There was no peeping or any sound coming from anywhere, apart from a singing Robin on top of the Centre's main indoor building. I peered in, there she was, sitting upright on a blanket of ice that had covered her pool. She looked excited and impatient to see me but didn't make a sound. I grabbed her some food from the bucket and headed to the middle of her enclosure. She quickly followed, after slipping and fumbling on the ice like an Otter version of Bambi. Before taking the food from me, she nuzzled her head onto my knees, very uncharacteristic behaviour for her; she'd usually grab her meal and then ask questions later. That was the first time she seemed to be happier to see me, rather than her breakfast.

I remember one day, in the late afternoon sun, just sitting on her small wooden bridge, she came over and sat near me, curled up and just gazed almost aimlessly around at her surroundings. I just stared up at the floating clouds as a passing Peacock butterfly caught my eye. I looked down to my right and she was doing the same. Drawn in by the movements of the small floating insect, her head was weaving about as the butterfly moved around. The brightly coloured butterfly landed on a single Thistle amongst a patch of Nettles and the inquisitive Squeaks excitedly bounded over toward the butterfly. As she approached, the Peacock spread her wings fully and flashed the false eyes on her wings, a beautiful defence to ward off potential predators. Squeaks was having none of it and approached ever nearer until the butterfly felt she was too close and folded her wings and became almost black as she hid her bold colours away, before launching once more up into the sky and out of sight. Squeaks twitched her nose before sitting upright and staring upward again. I couldn't help but feel for her. As much as I loved watching her, I couldn't help thinking she must feel sad not to be free of this enclosure; it's all she would've known, but I could imagine her in a social group, swimming down large rivers as a wild Otter.

As time went on, I found myself spending more of my time with her, just sitting with her in a place of calm. We were almost opposites as she craved freedom but, unknowingly, she had given me mine.

Long summer days turned into autumn. As the months went on, the bouncy Otter became slightly more lethargic and less vocal; as she was rescued a long time ago from a private collection, no-one really knew how old she was, but she'd been at the Centre for at least seven years when I arrived. Something wasn't quite right with her. The days had shortened, and the weather was turning colder.

With the colder months approaching, I started spending even more of my time with her as I didn't really want her to be alone whilst also getting my comfort from her too. Her holt was again packed up with straw and the blanket reappeared for her to curl up inside. I went to check on her last thing at night and then again at first light. She always bounded out when I called, but at night I would have thoughts of a time when I would call her out of her sleeping area, and she wouldn't appear.

Just before Christmas she had perked up, she was looking and sounding a lot more like her old self. I was so happy to see her bouncing about and rolling in the water like she did before. A lot of animals have impressive movement but the way she rolled in the water, almost as one with it, was mesmerising. Despite her return to form, I knew deep down it was just a front, that something was underlying.

Sometimes, late into the evening, I could hear her whimpering, pining to herself amongst the various other animals calling, like the chattering Foxes or the screeching Barn Owls. It was sad to hear her, and, on more than one occasion, I would sneak over to see her. I'd just lean over the sloped barrier and stay there, for an hour sometimes. As soon as I would appear, her aching cry would stop, and she would joyfully peep at me for a few minutes until she settled. Usually, before an hour was up, she'd wander back into her little hole in the box for some more rest. Sometimes she'd head into the box and turn herself around and poke her head out to see if I was still there, which I often was. Even though it would be mostly dark, I could still see that little twinkle in her eyes. Over the next few months, as the winter very gradually turned to spring, the Crab Apple blossom made its appearance on the tree that overhung her home.

Then, one day my fear was realised. I approached her enclosure with a whistle but there to be no squeaking or peeping. I peeked my head over the wooden frame and called again and it was met with silence. I felt my heart stop for a second as I jumped the frame and tapped on her sleeping chamber, still nothing. I lifted the lid and there she was, lying on her side and seemingly breathing with a shallow breath with her eyes partly open. She tilted her head to look at me briefly then rested it again on the warm straw that lined her home. It would turn out to be the last time I saw her look at me. I stroked her back and she closed her eyes like she was comforted by my touch. I left to get help and make a call to the local vet. I was only gone a few minutes before I returned to her enclosure. She lay there, still, with her eyes firmly shut. I stayed with her for an hour until the vet arrived, hoping and praying this wouldn't be the last hour I would spend with her.

The vet arrived and gave her a quick examination before taking her immediately back to the practice. We were told within a few hours that it wasn't good news and to prepare for the worst. She was kept in overnight, and that night, for me, was horrible. Thoughts of her wandered around in my mind as I struggled to sleep. The next morning, I carried on with my duties at the Centre, feeding the other animals and cleaning out the Aviaries. Walking past her empty enclosure was heart wrenching. I spent the morning praying that my phone would never ring. Then, midway through the afternoon it happened. I crumbled like a scrunched up leaf onto the floor of the Deer enclosure; my worst fears were realised. She'd gone!

She was quite old and suffering from kidney stones and various tumours that she'd been carrying for some time; animals have a habit of hiding any weakness until it's too late. It was the best thing for her as she was obviously hiding the pain inside. I wished she was still here. I knew it was for the best - it just didn't feel that way.

I stared aimlessly into her home, a home which I helped to build. I hope she enjoyed her time in it while she could. The tears falling down my face and onto the wooden frame are ones of sadness and relief as I knew she was now out of pain. I can still see her deep hazel brown eyes staring up at me from the corner of her home. My time with her was on loan, I just didn't know how short that time would be or how much she would change everything.

I knew after that day that I could no longer carry on at the Sanctuary. I think the end came at the right time for both of us. That day was horrible, I lost the little Otter who ignited something inside me, and in return, I made her feel part of a social group again, even if it was just the two of us.

I went to the fallen tree by the river that day - I knew it was a place I'd be welcome. I just sat there and reflected on where I was and where I wanted to go from here.

I've never looked back since and I'll continue my journey with her. Every time I go in search of her British cousins. I'll take her with me, give her the sort of journey she never really had - she was captive, but I hope she felt free. Every Otter I've seen, and will ever see, I'll remember her and see her in the eyes of every single one.

I needed to get out, to explore, to track down the wild Otter, the creature I've loved since I was a boy.

None of the Otters, or the stories that go with them would ever have happened without her.

The Torch

I hide behind an old broken farm gate, in between the leftover cereal crops and the untamed nettles. I can see a few distant, dark golden-brown shapes lying flat to the ground. The sky is in a peaceful state with one of the last survivors of the dinosaur era whirling high up and away into the darkening sky, freckled with tiny clouds. The Dragonfly has disappeared out of sight and there's a hum of bees over the short grasses in the field behind me. A Skylark sings with the sound of summer with its melodic vocal high above and a wavering Blue butterfly quarters his territory just above the meadow.

It's a peaceful early summer's evening but it's about to be anything but as the calm is broken by the beautiful Hare frantically chasing another one from one side to the other, entangled together in a blur of russet brown before resting, until the next flurry begins, twisting and turning up the short grass as they try to outdo the other. It's quietened down and the sight of the few remaining Hares with their pointed, ink dipped ears raised up high, is a magical sight of an animal rapidly disappearing from the landscape.

I leave the Hares to box it out before the night falls and head to the meadow that runs parallel with the river behind. I weave in and out of the sparse Wood Anemones and Lesser Celandines and hear the distant high-pitched sound of the beautiful blue bird. He's calling through his territory one last time before the light loses its battle with the night.

I reach the riverside just in time to see the tiny blue arrow flash past me on the other side of the water. He settles behind an Ivy drenched Oak that holds itself over the river. I can just about make out the dip of his tail through the leaves. His day seems to be done but for others it's time for them to wake up as the moon rises from the distant farm fields.

I follow the river into the wood, on the edges a carpet of blue, white and yellow smothers the green floor. The wood feels alive with all sorts of sounds coming from each corner. It's like a concert is about to start; all the orchestra are lining up ready, the musicians and singers are on their platform in place, the conductor has put the finishing touches to his little bow tie and he's just waiting patiently for an audience.

Rodents scrape and scurry in the undergrowth as a Robin sings as loudly as he can from a stump in the middle. He's joined by a random vocal performance by a Blackcap with his scratchy song. A sweet and melodic Yellowhammer trills away from the Hawthorn bushes on the outside of the wood.

I'm Settling into the heart of the wood, trying to blend in unnoticed. The trees have a way of making me feel as though I'm being watched, but in a comforting way. I find the perfect spot in which to settle. I relocate some fallen Holly leaves, press my cheek firmly against the soft earth and scrunch my arms and legs into the entanglement of the old Oak roots.

The gentle dusk cacophony comes to an end as the Blackbird delivers its melodic goodnight song. I feel completely at one with my surroundings as my heart beats slower and in rhythm with the old wood. The crepuscular creatures are about to make their awaited appearance.

When the wood senses something's arriving its mood changes and it makes me aware of it; it could be an obvious sound of breaking twigs, a noise coming through a bush or an alarm call from a Wren or other another small bird. This time though it's a short, peeped alarm from a Robin perched low down on the end of an exposed branch about forty feet away. I can't see any movements from below the perch, then, a silhouette of two triangular ears and a pointed snout - it reveals itself to be a Fox coming out of the shadows and into the last of the light coming through the almost full canopy of leaves.

The Robin halts his alarms and flies high up into the higher branches of the tree. The Fox edges in my direction, but so far, is unaware of me scrunched up amongst the tangled roots. He stops briefly and points his nose up to taste the air, he seems content and carries on his jaunt. He has a purposeful but gentle motion as he strides through the wood and out of my sight and the calm falls around me again.

For half an hour I look through the corridor of trees and stare intently at a few scattered Badger holes that are a short distance away. The holes are deeply dug into the ground with huge scraped out and flattened entrances. The dark is creeping quickly through the wood and the holes are getting harder to focus on. After a few more minutes I finally hear a sniffling sound coming from the biggest hole and I hold my breath. I don't need to wait any more as I can just see the tip of the nose making that sniffly sound; it's grainy black and flanked by a cluster of whiskers. Its head raises up and is in full view with its iconic double black stripes whilst keeping its body still and close to the ground. He looks fully aware and is using all his senses to detect if there is any danger above ground, including me. The older dominant male of the sett has the task to make sure all is safe for the rest of the group and, once he has done his checks, he will communicate that all is well for them to come out too. He tentatively creeps out and heads in the direction of another hole a few metres away. Hopefully I have gone undetected and I will soon be rewarded by one of Britain's most recognisable mammals.

A few minutes pass by with only a call of an early Tawny Owl to break the silence, and then, out from the second hole is the first Badger, looking at ease as he tastes the crisp air. He's joined by a second that's being almost pushed out by a boisterous third who looks smaller than the others and is one of this year's cubs, bouncing around but sticking close to its mother. Eventually, seven animals are out and scuffling with each other, between the almost endless amounts of scratching, mainly on themselves, but occasionally scratching the back of one another. They have not noticed the creature watching on, still wedged in the entangled roots just beyond them. As they finish their last scratch, they gather for what looks like a team meeting before heading in line towards the ever-darkening open field and they are gone.

I start to detangle myself from the roots and as the blood comes back, I wipe the dirt and leaves from my face and smile as that was a wonderful and secret encounter. I wait a few minutes then head out of the woods through the corridor of Silver Birch and weave through the nettles and into the open of the pathway. The riverbank opens-up in front of me. An isolated Ash tree on the far side leaves a dark and mysterious silhouetted shape reflected onto the river which is now the colour of the twilight blue. The air has begun to turn night-time cold and, with the flow of the river in front of me, I find a spot to sit beside; a good clutch of Bullrushes. I've seen Otter prints pressed on the mud by the shallows before so figure it's as good a place as any to try to see one.

Armed with a torch that already seems to be struggling and with my wildly over-the-top expectations, I start to aim the light up and down the short section of water the light will reach. The places where the light won't quite reach, are the spots I imagine things are. I convince myself that all the ripples from fish and the occasional floating branch is an Otter.

The sound of two Tawny owls calling back and forth to each other in the direction of the wood I came from is the only sound. An Otter could come past at any moment and I constantly count down from ten to zero hoping that will be the moment. I'm not sure it really works like that, but it keeps me amused, nonetheless.

There's a short, sharp call coming from an Ash tree across the river, it sounds vaguely like the call Squeaks used to make when she was begging for food but with a lot less intensity. I wait in complete darkness, with my torch turned off with an attempt to not scare off the animal making the noise. It seems to be getting louder and nearing the water's edge, so I flick the light on and shine it over towards the bank. The light barely trickles across and just catches the line as, casting it in a dim orange light, there's no movement around the bank. The noise stops as I wave the torch around in the hope of seeing some eye shine. I turn the torch off again and wait in my slumped position beside the rushes. The sharp call starts up again whilst I try to figure out if I'm hearing it my head. It calls for a few minutes until I turn the torch on again and aim it across the river, it sounds even more like an Otter than at the start and I can now see the Otter in my mind. A slight splash coming from the near bank sends a shiver down my back but still I can't see anything. Then, all of a sudden, the pitch of the call changes to more of a choking bird. There it is, on the lower branches of the Ash tree, a Starling; the dark bird just sits there and opens its beak and repeats the squeaky call. He looks more than half asleep and I wonder if they do it without knowing, or as a contact call to others roosting nearby.

Another hour goes by without a flicker in the water or a sound as the Starling hasn't called for a while. The torch with its rechargeable batteries is only stretching half the distance as earlier and not quite reaching to the far places by the roots. A Crow further upstream calls out, as loud as it is random, and scares me half to death. My thoughts that it was disturbed by an Otter send me into a scene that the Otter, in its hurry to evade the calling Crow, ends up coming out the river and sitting next to me, and after a short conversation, he slips back into the water. Very wishful thinking but I have spent a long time watching the seemingly empty water.

The dark sky is retreating with the oncoming lighter blue appearing in the east as it washes away the stars and the moon. It's been a long but very beautiful evening in the company of the night river. Just to attempt to see a wild Otter feels like some sort of achievement. I knew my chances were ridiculously low, but I still enjoyed my evening by the river side.

The Ash across the river becomes brighter as the light rapidly changes the landscape. Birds start chattering up and down the river as it becomes light and, as dawn breaks on the river, a gliding mist rolls just above the surface of the water.

The Kingfisher from the night before is up and making the world aware of this fact. His high-pitched whistle is carrying sharply over the water. He dashes up-river before turning around at the bend and whizzing back towards me. His call seems intense as he glides at speed past me and down river; I can still hear his call as the flash of blue moves out of sight.

The burnt yellow sun peeks just above the old farmhouse behind the field, I can't wait to feel its warmth on my skin. It's been a long and sometimes cold night by the river. I leave the water's edge for another day and head tiredly away from the river and over the broken fence that leads into the open field filled with Rabbits and sun-kissed grassy dew. I wipe my tired eyes and blink from the brightness of the very early sun that's rapidly climbing the sky.

A Fox is making his way across the maze of Rabbits and Sheep to the other side in the direction of the wood. He stops in the middle and sits upright; the sun catches him and changes his dark coat into a bright rusty red. He stays there for a few minutes just staring aimlessly into the sun; occasionally he scratches his ears with his front paws and opens his mouth to yawn as fully as possible. He trots off through a gap in the fence leaving a trail of paw prints behind in the dew. I head through the gate and up the steep track that leads to my door and head straight for the kettle.

Sometimes you've just got to put yourself out there and immerse yourself in nature.

Bird song fills the wood, flowers line the riverside, small animals rummage around in the leaf litter. Squabbling Badgers, wandering Foxes, darting Kingfishers, boxing Hares and everything else that made the afternoon into the night and back to the morning again - so much of an adventure. I always get rewarded by something beautiful and unexpected when I'm outdoors.

I'm still determined to catch a glimpse of my first wild Otter, but for now, I'll have to settle for a great night out by the river.

First Wild Otter

Leaving the mainland behind shrouded in clouds with fine rain sweeping in like a sandstorm across the sea, I pass by small rocky islands with just a handful of worn, washed-out white cottages on them.

The sea looks like it goes on forever and is greeted in the middle by the sound of an old guard of a lighthouse with a few Seals lounging around on its rocky shore. Every one of the Seals is marked differently, ranging from mottled black and grey spots to a deep blue with a pale face. Some of them take to the water as I pass by; they bob up and down like bobbing corks and stare longingly up at me.

A couple of Gannets wheel high up into the sky adding a flash of brilliant white to the concrete grey sky. A small passage of Auks shoots by like little winged bullets; the dark-backed birds flicker black to white as they twist and turn above the angry waves.

The further I go, the less dreary it becomes as the deep-blue sky breaks through the thin wall of grey and pockets of light seep through. More and more seabirds stream up the channels as the island comes into view, with the shape of the distinctive hills outlining the landmass.

A large raft of Eider float on the surface, the brown females outnumber the white plumaged males three to one. A lone male Great Northern Diver sits just off the raft of sea ducks. I catch a glimpse of his reptilian like white patterned markings on his mostly black body; his head is coal black and there's a flicker of a red snake-like eye. He arches his body over and, in one motion, dives under the surface near the drifting Eider.

The island draws ever nearer, and the distinctive shape of a regal castle sits very defensive on its mound, surrounded by a great arched bay and a cliff that looks man-made but has been shaped over time by the sea.

Broken stone walls mark the start of the land and a mass of summer green trees rise from the shoreline. Past the tree line is a dauntingly beautiful mountain, sat ominously in low, misty cloud. The natural cathedral looms over the forest and coastline below.

A burst of rain from the heavy clouds high up to my left and beautiful shards of sunlight pour through a gap and combine to produce a vivid rainbow over the harbour like a warm, friendly welcome mat. Its bright colours arc over the port against a mosaic of layered trees with a few houses dotted around its base.

Stepping onto the island I instantly feel welcomed. I'm not sure how to describe it but it feels right, it feels like I belong, in a place I've never been.

For a few minutes I sit on the harbour wall and gaze back from where I came. The gloomy mass of clouds is still looming over the mainland and looks another world away, but still close somehow.

There's a small gathering of Turnstone on the pebbled shoreline; they sit still with their beaks tucked into their upper wings. The five of them blend in against the rocks and are only visible when they fidget and shuffle.

I turn my back on the mainland to face this brand-new playground ahead of me. I leave the harbour and head up, over mainly upland fields and Bracken plastered hills covered in Highland Cows. Isolated Lochans dot the landscape and sparkle in the new sun of the afternoon with a metallic sheen. I'm trying to turn every Mallard on the small Lochs into a Diver and every flying Buzzard into a soaring Golden Eagle, none of which happens, despite how much I try. The clouds seem to pass by in time-lapse mode as the wind picks up and blows them frantically across the sky. Every direction has a view to wonder at and I can't wait to start exploring this new land.

The road winds down a steep pass that snakes around rocky outcrops and an old weather-beaten graveyard that stares down over the small village below. I follow the track that takes me to a traditional old stone bridge that rises over the river that empties into a huge tidal sea Loch that dominates as far as the meeting with the Atlantic Ocean. High banks of Heather sit either side of the path that leads towards my home for a week.

My base is a wooden A-frame style dwelling that's hidden well by overgrown shrubs and a stack of chopped wood. Without invitation, I head straight to the large open-plan window which looks straight down onto a couple of pools, a small patch of Reeds and the river that leads to the Loch and the little bridge that I've just ambled over. The sun is struggling to force its way through the clouds that are covering much of the sky.

The day is long in the middle of the summer but now it's entering its last section as it falls faster in the direction of the dark sloped hills behind the Loch. The last of the remaining streaks of light flow with the stream and pour out onto the waiting sea Loch that's glistening between the grey.

The colours of the landscape seem more vibrant here, like they did when I was young when I used to explore evergreen fields and woods with mystical trees; the feeling that anything is possible, but nothing on this scale. Everything seems so much bigger.

It's the widest I've ever seen the sky and it looks like half the world lies in front of me, a world filled with wondrous possibilities. I'd seen these places in my mind a thousand times and daydreamed of how I would see an Otter for the first time; sitting waiting as the Otter meanders up-river at dawn or swimming around in calm sea waters as the sun sets behind. Dreams are made to be perfect but real life rarely is.

The sky is brewing up some fierce-looking clouds and the light is fading fast from the hills but it's a crossover light when nature moves in two directions; one to sleep after a long day and one waking up to face the night.

Ghosting in from the ever-increasing gloom is a bird that lights up its surroundings, he angles his wings and floats down the slope on softly coloured grey wings. The tips look like they've been soaked in black ink, brilliant flashes of white come between the two when he leisurely twists in the air. It's my first wild Hen Harrier I've seen and the best descriptions in books don't do it any kind of justice.

The clouds have a stronghold above him, and the rain is falling steadily and being blown about across the hillside, as is the lonesome Harrier. He rows his wings quicker and quicker to push through and around the wind before settling on an old farm gate. He sits there hunched up like an Owl as the wind blows against his back and ruffles his feathers in all directions. In the time it's taken him to settle, he's off again, gliding across the Bracken covered hillside and away below the darkened slope.

The clouds have thickened even more and turned almost charcoal black, still furiously moving across the sky and beyond the distant hill line as the raindrops fall against the window with a pinch of summer.

My eyes are drawn immediately to a splash on one of the furthest pools near the bridge. I can't see any movement as the pool returns to a stillness. My eyes are straining in the fading light to scan the pools and the river. I look in complete disbelief at what looks like an Otter sitting just above the surface like a piece of wood. It's a distance away as it disappears into the tall grasses that line the pool. I'm trying to convince myself that what I saw wasn't just a dog having a paddle with an owner nearby and that they would come into view at some point. No-one appeared.

I'm too excited and I need to know either way what I'd seen and there's still a bit of light left in this day. I throw on my coat, waterproof trousers and reach for my cap, straight out the door and down the slope towards the pools. I scramble over a broken fence that tears a piece out of my trousers. I hop across the squelchy bog that tries to take my shoe captive as I plunge deep into its spongy surface. It releases me eventually as I reach another fence, before finding myself eye level with the first pool and follow its edges towards the second pool where the creature was. The light is really struggling against the drops of rain that have become heavy and noisy as they hit the shallow surface of the pool. A large patch of Vetch, Thistle and tall Wild Grass acts as a partition between the two pools.

I kneel-down in between the mixed flora, gently bend back a few pieces of thick grass, peer through and wait. The pool is empty and devoid of life. The far Reeds look weighed down under the pressure from the rain and the sea Loch and the surrounding woodland loses all colour as dark grey dominates the scape. My near view still has splashes of colour from the Thistle flower and the Yellow Iris but even they are fighting against the ever-darkening light.

I wait and watch for movement amongst the Reeds down to the opening of the Loch but there's none, just a lonesome Heron perched, with his head tucked down low into his folded wings on a jagged piece of driftwood on the other side of the bridge. No Otter or dog to be seen. I doubt myself and question if I'd seen anything at all.

The rain and the light are getting the better of me. I turn away dampened and a little disheartened. As I squelch back through the Sphagnum Moss, a short-whistled squeak comes from the direction of the pool. I crawl slowly and sodden back through the grasses and bend the curtain of grass as slowly as I can under these hyper-excited circumstances. The Reeds on the far side rustle and move in a way that only a large mammal could cause, and then, through a gap in the stems, dark brown, sleek fur appears. An Otter ....

I can't make him out, just a brown mass behind the first line of Reeds. I wait, almost too excited to be staying still. A glimpse of its head or a flick of its tail is all it'll take. Then the nose of the Otter pushes through the Reeds as he comes out into the open in all his full Otter glory. I could see his long tail, flat head and his oversized brilliant whiskers with the tiniest flicker of light in his eyes. He ambles towards the water and slips under the dark surface. I hold my breath for a few seconds. The rain is now lashing against the pool's surface, mesmerisingly, bouncing the water upwards as I wait for the Otter to re-emerge. The ten seconds or so until he reappears seems to last an eternity. His head sits above the water for a second, before almost instantly arching over and diving under again.

I don't think I can be any wetter, and the rain, now leaking through the small hole the fence ripped out of my trousers.

He swirls around and around the small pool, but I know it's not big enough to keep him here for long and the dark sky was close to claiming victory. I think the weather is on my side as the Otter seems oblivious to my presence. He swims around in a circle seemingly giving chase to his own tail just like the way Squeaks did in her muddy little pool; all his body in one motion as he stirs up the water. It's frantic, but also graceful, as the water and the Otter merge. Then a moment of calm and still as he paddles to the side of the pool, scrambles through the muddy shallows between the watery grass that lines that side of the pool. The Otter sleeks fully out of the water and shakes from his head to the tip of his tail as it flicks upwards.

For a moment the Otter just sits still giving me the chance to stare as his back's turned. He's taking a few seconds to do nothing before re-joining his manic nature. He turns and looks straight at the oddly shaped object wedged behind the grass, and, for the briefest second, I'm sure he knows I'm there. He exhales deeply enough that I can hear him; it sounds like a sigh, then grunts twice in a grumpy fashion before facing away. He bounds across the wet mix of grasses and moss with a motion that looks smooth but also out of time. He sniffs low down at a randomly placed moss-covered rock and disappears over a grassy bank that hides the upper part of the adjoining river that leads towards the large open Loch. The rain isn't falling like normal it's now coming down as one light but smothering mass of water with a summery warmth to it. The Otter who's probably close to the mouth of the Loch by now, has taken the last of the light with him and left me soaked to the bone but given me my first glimpse into the life of a wild Otter.

I get up from the vegetation and wander back towards my cabin, every step feels light and playful and even the damaged fence is hurdled like I'm floating on air. I joyfully greet a singing Blackbird but a little too loudly for his liking; he flies hastily away into a dark smattering of Rowan trees just beside the main track.

I've seen many beautiful wild animals, but this was the one that captivated me above all others, and I knew it was just the beginning of my journey with the Otter.

The Frozen Cloak

The field is dressed in a frozen white cloak whilst the moon teases me through the thinned-out Birch wood on the hill and tickles the few remaining clouds that are a wintry pink. Her night's work is done and now she's setting before the sun rises. I get my first glimpse of the river in dreamlike stillness as it leaves the wood towards the weir.

Walking across the icy field I leave a darkened imprint on the white which maps out my meandering route. The wooden gate is plastered in silky frozen spiderwebs that glisten in the morning light; I push through the gate and leave my mark on the pale wood behind me. The water is passing under the old bridge in a dreamy slow state and, just like me, is in no hurry at all. I step onto the old brickwork of the bridge that leads to an island in the river that's mainly used by grazing cattle and the occasional weekend fisherman. The sun has not even climbed above the eastern wooded hill and already I'm watching a couple of early returning Sand Martins with beautiful light chocolate brown bodies and milky chests fly low up and down the river - they've just arrived back from their arduous journey from Africa. It always amazes me that something with a heart the size of theirs has the capacity to make the journey and do it every year.

Looking down from the bridge I can really see how the river moves from behind the wood and flows around the island towards the weir with ease. I duck my head under a Weeping Willow tree and skirt the water's edge, looking back at the emerging leaves and catkin drapes from the tree. I can remember that view from when I was a child. It looks like the tree sits on an island within an island from this angle and has never changed; I'm not sure I've changed all that much either. I sit on the frosty bank a hundred metres or so down and look back at the old bridge and the Willow.

It's March and it's that time when winter is still clinging on, but Spring is breaking free of its hold and pushing pieces of new life through. Birds that were quiet are now reaching their peak with bird song flooding from every tree, fence post and water side. Sounds of Robin, Blue Tit and Great Tit combine beautifully with Blackbird, Blackcap and Song Thrush but it's the Wren that dominates the sound and they are singing from everywhere. That beautiful trill is bleeding into me like nothing else. I catch sight of one on the post that sits in the shallow water of the river and it delivers a perfect rendition of its tune which bounces off the sides of the steadily flowing river. He raises his tail and shakes his entire body, giving the performance absolutely everything in that ten seconds. He flies across to the lone Ash tree that sits at the water's edge at the end of the island and repeats his performance.

A male Blackbird sits on top of the same tree and belts out his soft melodic song as the Wren flies up-river and into the scrub. Now a Grey Wagtail, with its bouncy flight, lands on the small patch of mud on the riverbank opposite me. He's the latest one competing for the limelight, armed with a spitfire grey and soft sulphur yellow, bobbing and flicking his tail as he forages in the shallows. He flies down river and lands on the middle of the old bridge and calls out into the morning. Rabbits come out to play onto the quickly thawing field as I watch my footprints disappear as white turns to green; they run and weave around the impressive amount of Mole hills. Clearly the Mole has been working overtime through the night. Playtime stops abruptly and the Rabbits scatter like crumbs from a table as an imposing early Buzzard lands midway up the field on a fence post. The Buzzard sits and waits, staring out intently on the area where the Rabbits disappeared but there's no sign of them. He opens his wings against the backdrop of the ancient Oak tree and glides effortlessly in the direction of the large Pine trees landing high up on a bare and smooth looking branch. He's still glaring down at the field, playing the long game of patience. He'll wait his time until the Rabbits feel the danger has passed and it's safe to come out.

Something else is stirring behind the old wood.

The sun is creeping in between the trees and peeping out through a thin veil of morning mist. The mist spills down from the wood onto the field and finally touches the surface of the river. Before long, the sun has climbed above the last of the tall trees and rained its light over everything in the river valley, turning the ghostly mist into a golden sheet across the surface of the water and illuminating the old bridge. Just up to the right is the weir that sits just down from the bridge and a fed-up looking Heron waits patiently on the edge, his head sinks into his shoulders, his beak pokes towards the water expectantly. The motionless Heron is joined by an elegant Little Egret that floats down river and over the weir, dressed in an all-white frilly gown and lands opposite the crestfallen looking Heron at the river's edge and starts to preen it's feathers with its pointy black bill. After a quick preen of her immaculate plumage she flies low downstream and settles on the tip of an old wooden jetty.

The water in front of me is going at its own casual pace and makes no noise. By contrast, the sound from the weir is a crashing filtering noise, but not unpleasant. Walking further away from the weir towards the end of the island, it's obvious an Otter has passed recently as a fresh spraint sits on top of a prominent mound of grass, near the muddy shallows; it has that wonderful smell that instantly makes me smile, maybe he or she is still around.

This tip of the little grassy island is perfect to gaze right down the barrel of the river at its widest point. A pair of Great Crested Grebes briefly showcase their dancing talents with synchronised dives and frilly head rolls before swimming beyond the bend and out of sight. The trees on either side are beginning to dress themselves with an armour of vibrant green leaves and the last of the snowdrops are giving way to the bright yellow Lesser Celandines on the bank. The light from the sun suddenly disappears as a bold cloud passes across its path and is joined on either side by more incoming clouds. The trees lose their colour immediately to a duller, toned-down version that is still beautiful.

The water is still calm and it's not long before the first raindrops start to fall shattering the reflective river and creating dreamy patterns on the surface. Before the clouds fully burst, I head back up towards the bridge and seek shelter under the Willow resting my back against the smooth trunk, surrounded by the long drapes of the Willow which act like partial curtains sheltering me, just enough to still give a clear view of the river. Just before the drop of the weir the water is at its calmest point and the Heron remains on the weir's edge looking much more animated now with his head up and neck stretched out towards the furiously cascading water. The rain is falling steadily and dripping off the new leaves of the Willow and onto the river's surface. The rain starts beating down heavier and makes a slight drumming sound as it hits the water under the Willow. I remain surprisingly dry, which can't be said of the Heron that looks bedraggled and is stubbornly staying put, waiting for his moment to catch breakfast. A pair of a whiter than white Mute Swans swim level with each other under the bridge and forage on grasses on the watery slope; they've already started constructing a nest up-river for the season ahead. The Heron suddenly screeches and swings his head from side to side as if something is beneath the water. He shuffles a little way back from the edge and looks rattled, standing there with a stern glare into the water. Through the chaos of the choppy water at the bottom of the weir I clearly can't see what he can. After a few minutes of upright posing at the river he resumes his first position and arrows his beak downwards and, quick as a flash, he has a decent sized Eel hanging out of his sunshine yellow bill. His patience and stubbornness have been rewarded, and so has mine. Despite the downpour there's so much life to watch and it's changed so fast. It feels like such a long time since the field was dressed in white as it's now drenched in dark green from the heavy rain.

There's a high-pitched peep echoing up-river and over the weir to where I'm sitting. I don't need a second listen to know this is the male Kingfisher on his morning territorial patrol. He glides low over the surface like a little blue jet plane and comes into land on an exposed piece of branch that must have floated downstream and been lodged on the side. It makes for a perfect perch for the colourful little fisher king. His head bobs up and down as he adjusts his position on the branch just up the river. He's not looking down at the river, or looking for fish, he's scanning with his deep hazel eyes for any intruding males in his territory. He looks on high alert as a female darts past him making no sound and he launches off the perch leaving a blue trail behind and peeps loudly behind her. I'm presuming this is his mate who has been sharing the territory up-river as there's no aggression between them. He catches up with her before the bend and they are out of sight. I can still hear the faint call from the Kingfisher as it carries over the water, then silence again.

The rain has begun to ease off and the clouds become lighter as the late winter sun fights hard to break through, contrasting light and dark. There's that high-pitched peep again as the Kingfisher once again rounds the bend, shoots under the bridge and glides low onto the branch once more. He puffs out his autumnal orange chest and angles his head, showing off the iridescent blue jewels in his crown and the lightening streak of electric blue running down his back, right to the tip of his tail, which contrasts dramatically with the much duller background of discarded Ash leaves and overgrown Bramble. With the water more settled from the easing of the rain, he begins a staring contest with the flat, shallow water underneath him, gazing completely transfixed on any ripple and every tiny splash from the raindrops, while keeping fully focused and holding his head motionless as he sits five feet above. I'm not sure if it's the anticipation but it feels as if the clocks have stopped at this moment, as it seems like forever and the skip of a heartbeat rolled into one. Then, at the blink of an eye, he's dropped head-first in a blur of orange and blue, hitting through the surface with force, slicing through the water and leaving a sizeable splash behind him as he submerges himself below. Within seconds, and before the water settles, he emerges, pounding his wings as hard as they'll beat until he's clear of the water and pointing upward towards the branch from where he came. His tiny blood red feet grasp onto the exposed perch and lodged in his beak is what looks like a Stickleback. He turns it around to face outwards. carefully trying not to drop the fish in the process, then has a quick shake to get rid of any remaining water and flies up-river holding the fish firmly as he goes. He's taking it to the female as a gift, as part of their courtship to solidify their bond.

The sky is now split into two with dark clouds and rain lingering to my right. On my left, the clouds have dispersed to let the sun cast its light down, lighting up the willow I'm still sitting under and showing off the powdery yellow catkins, turning the river into a mix of all tones of morning blue. The Heron calls out his alarm screech abruptly and stretches his big grey wings, flying heavily down river and up, over to beside a small pool in the field, calling as he goes. I catch the quickest glimpse of what looks like an Otter's tail in the bubbling water of the weir. It's a mass of swirling chaotic water and it's hard to see anything through it, maybe it's what got the Heron so upset. I'm still waiting under the drapes of the Willow and intently gazing in the calm either side of the weir.

The rain is falling lightly onto the river, then clambering through the fast-flowing water of the weir is the Otter I've been waiting for. He pushes through the final bit of waterfall-like cascade and stops briefly to look around before sliding into the still river near the side of the bank. He's under the water but a trail of bubbles on the surface map out his unpredictable route. Then he's up and his head is just about visible under the overhanging Bramble, chomping away at something. I can't see through the thick leaves what it is. Then he's under again and heading towards the middle of the river, only about fifty feet away from the base of the Willow. He comes up much closer, about twenty feet away, and is as still as the water. He stares at the Willow, puffs out his cheeks and makes a loud sighing noise, sinking his body underneath so it's just his little ears, his broad flat nose and a face full of whiskers visible, continuing to gaze in my direction. There is no movement for almost half a minute until his nose twitches and he dives underneath again, vanishing this time with no trail of bubbles to follow, before reappearing slightly further up-river. He begins rolling about in the middle. It looks like he's playing with the water, swirling around and around then he makes a line for a muddy bank just to my left, between me and the old bridge, leaving that distinctive v shape in the water behind him, gliding through the stillness of the water like no other. He reaches the muddy shallows and wades out of the water up onto a sloped grassy bank. I have a partial view as the Willow drapes obscure him from my eye-line. He begins having a good scratch of his head before rolling onto his back and clawing at his pale brown stomach. Two Mallards are heading in his direction and I wait, expecting a reaction from them, but they pass within feet of him while the Otter continues grooming himself vigorously. The Ducks paddle quietly by without any commotion. After the shallows, the two Drakes smack their wings against the murky water until they are airborne in a blur of chestnut brown, pale grey, oily bluish green and a vibrant flash of blue on the wings. One frantically flies high above the river and just clears the bridge whilst the other one flies straight, casting a reflection on the surface as he goes. They re-join each other on the other side and land a few hundred metres up, at the widest point. The Otter gets up from his grooming session and slides back into the water and makes his way up-river towards the bridge. I get up from my slouched position and leave the Willow behind, sticking close to the vegetation on the bank trying not to be seen, but the Otter's way out of sight and already past the bridge.

The day seems split into many pieces as the clouds peel away and late winter sun shines down again. Creeping past the bridge, keeping focused on the river, I can make out a splash coming from near the end of the island where the first sign of an Otter was. I creep ever closer using the base of a felled tree to mask my presence as the Otter is sniffing the spraint on the grassy mound in the shallows. He marks the mound with his own scent. Maybe this wasn't his territory as he seems agitated by the presence of the spraint and is looking around sniffing the air furiously, scratching around the base of the mound before slipping back into the river and turning around to snort loudly before diving under. I scramble through the long, wet grass to the end of the island.

The light is spectacular as the sun hits the damp trees and stretches across the river. Many birds have gathered in the middle of the river; the pair of Swans, the Mallards and Grebes are joined by a flock of Teal. The Otter emerges in the middle of them, much to the annoyance of the male Swan, who raises his wings and hisses at the unwelcome water dweller. The Otter disappears and comes back up just feet behind the Swan. I'm sure he thinks it's a game, but the Swan is not impressed and swipes his wing down towards the Otter, splashing up a mass of water. The Otter is too quick again. The Swan is very animated as he swims in circles watching the water for the Otter's reappearance but he's nowhere to be seen; the Swan won't rest until he's back in sight. He finally comes up and glides effortlessly through the golden light and out of the water on the far side of the river and scrambles onto the roots of an ancient looking Oak. He marks his territory and has a quick scratch then turns around and stares momentarily back at his world; the river, the bridge, the weir, the field and the woods all glowing in the midmorning sun. He scurries around the roots and up the darkened wooded bank and out of sight. His trip out for the night and early morning is done and soon mine will be too. I've watched so many changes to the mood of the morning from the white cloak and frosty field to the rain on the Willow and the stillness of the river and back to the sun again. I'm alone down here by the river but I'm never lonely surrounded by these wonderful creatures in this beautiful landscape and the ever-changing weather.

The Cubs

I walk up the dry and dusty track that leads to the old croft. Flocks of Twite and Crossbill cling to wired fences in the absence of trees and joyfully chatter amongst themselves, the latter having been blown over the sea from Scandinavia. The male Crossbills are painted in a bright rusty red and the females and youngsters are draped in a mushy olive green, their disproportionately large crossover bills looking like a kind of torture tool. I leave the flock of Finches on the wires and head further up the track.

I'm usually being blown around by the constant wind but today is a calm day; there's one of these every so often. The farm sits at the high point of the track and has views looking north and east and as far as the edge of the world. You could see a storm brewing for miles and watch it approach like an unwanted guest but met like a familiar old friend. So much here is reliant on the weather but the wildlife carries on regardless, whatever's thrown at them. Leaving the track through a shattered looking wooden gate and striding to the wildflower coated meadow that's bathed by a sun that seems to single out all the flowers individually and cast a spotlight on each and every one; the frilled pink of the Ragged Robin sitting next to Campions, Marsh Orchids and fairy-tale Dandelion clocks all have their place at centre stage. I walk straight through the middle of the field and find a place to sit and try and take in each, and every petal, and breathe in the floral scented sea breeze.

This small island in the middle of nowhere is so fertile and unspoilt that it creates these wonderful havens. A small, mystical stone circle, stands just before the slope to the sea, it's said to be a place where witches and fairies gather during the solstice and cause all sorts of mischief. The fairies supposedly would tie people's shoes together and tap at the windows. Thankfully they are not around today as I walk around it's edges.

I'd never seen the sea look so bright; it looks cartoon blue and the few clouds that were allowed in the sky were invited into the scape. This is the time of the never-ending light when actual darkness is a rare visitor to the night.

I leave the meadow and the stone circle and meander down toward the shore, following a Lichen drenched old stone wall. There were many holes in between the weather-beaten wall, some large enough to play peek-a-boo with anything on the other side, which happened on this occasion, to be a curious and scruffy looking sheep. I think she would've described me in the same way. A bright male Stonechat sits on guard at the end of the divide before the sea, looking quite proud of himself in his full summer uniform.

A handful of Puffins fly close to the bay, heading to find deeper water, I can just about make out their brightly coloured beaks. The funny little clowns of the sea will be back shortly with a beak full of Sand Eels to feed their ever-growing young. A pair of Little Ringed Plover patrol the entrance to the shore like little wind-up toys in full motion, they have a nest to defend nearby and are always looking alert for any danger. I sit on the lush grass and lean up against a rusty feeling stone wall and stare out across the bay to the tip of the rocks on the far cliffs across the wick, surveying everything and waiting for the tide to turn. The Sheep has got bored of playing hide and seek and has returned to the main flock up on the hill. The sound of Arctic Terns fills the air above me, their blood red bills leading the way as they look like they're about to attack anything in their territory. They're hovering ominously above my head with their angel white coat and coal black hood. They pass me by this time as I sit, motionless, and I breathe a sigh of relief. Through the chipping sound of the Wren working his way through the gaps in the wall, I can hear a sniffing and peeping call from a dip in a mound just up from the shore. I've never heard that sound before and so, I wait, and stare at the dip. After a few minutes a fluffy, pale brown head pops up, looks around, then disappears back into the dip again. I didn't get the best view, but it looks like an Otter cub. A Wheatear with its prominent white rump lands on the grassy mound and flits around between the white cover on the ridge. Suddenly two heads pop up and the little bird takes flight, heads to the stone wall where it displaces the Stonechat. It's two little Otter cubs rolling about together, nibbling each other's tails and nuzzling into the other one's soft but dense fur. Every now and then they squeak gently then duck out of sight and go silent as if they are waiting for something. Their mother must've left them to dry off whilst she forages the water for food. They look quite young and it doesn't look like they've been coming out of the natal holt for long. There's not a sight or sound from them for more than twenty minutes as I sit in anticipation of them to pop up again. Finally, a tiny paw raises up with an almost triumphant fist pump and it's quickly followed by two little heads popping above the dip. They are back up and they start rolling together again until they almost merge as one, small Otter mass. Peering at them through the small hole in the wall feels like staring into another world, a world I've been given a free pass to, a glimpse for a short while. Both hastily leave their little dip and bound buoyantly in the direction of the pebbled shore stopping on the edge looking a little unsure about the water and just stare out, huddled close to each other.

The slightly smaller cub lets out a squeak. Another peep from the youngster and they both send their high-pitched squeaks across the waves hoping that their mother will hear the call. It's not long before the calls start to sound agitated and desperate as they are met with no response. I feel for the pair of them, and in some part, it breaks my heart but I'm sure she won't be far.

They walk together up and down the shoreline sniffing at the rocks and scratching at the exposed sandy patches. They claw away but she won't be found under a rock or in the sand. They seem reluctant to enter the water and slump together behind a small rock that barely hides them. The cries have become less frequent as they rest, helpless on the shore. All they can do is wait. The grey figure of a Hooded Crow approaches the motionless cubs, hopping and edging towards them, being careful not to make a sound. An eye from the smaller cub flickers and she springs into action and runs with a scrambling motion towards the Crow who briefly stands its ground before being forced to take flight by the boisterous little cub. The other one follows and for a few minutes, they bounce and play on the rocks; they've distracted themselves from the squeaking and search for their mother, if only for a short while. A short peep from a nearby Rock Pipit seems to start them off again but this feels more agonising for them and their cries sound even more heart-breaking. The calls suddenly quicken and slightly changes pitch turning into an excited cry as both gaze low over the water, and there she is, approaching low but still distant, just with her head above the tide.

Both dip their front paws into the shimmering water and suddenly they've forgotten their fear, they plunge in and paddle as quick as their little legs will take them in the direction of the oncoming Otter. The little Otters look like two bath toys whizzing across the surface. She's carrying what looks like a large Lumpsucker fish, mainly dark grey with a bright red colour on its belly. They are still peeping as they reach their mother and their excitement is obvious and a wonderful thing to watch. They jump and scramble all over her, but she's got the fish firmly in her mouth and won't release it until she meets the land, despite their best efforts to wrestle it away from her. She works her way through the maze of seaweed whilst being pursued closely by her young. She reaches the shallows and wades up and onto a flat, sun-bathed rock that looks carved just for this purpose. She places the fish down and shakes some of the water off her coat. The two cubs copy their mother and shake furiously as the water sprays in all directions. She finally relinquishes the fish to the cubs for them to scrap over, which they do. They pull and nip at the fish, each one taking a turn to run off with the prize. Bits of fish are flying in all directions and they're getting little pieces to munch through but trying desperately to keep it for themselves; so close and together until there's food, then it's about survival and first come, first served.

The female pays them no interest and leaves them to have their game. She slides back into the water and even though they were so longing to see her, they haven't even noticed she's disappeared again. She vanishes into the thick forest of weeds and leaves a beautifully reflected calm sea behind her. The flat rock is anything but as the cubs are still deadlocked in pursuit of the prize; neither one is backing down and in the midst of the fighting, the fish has been lost from their grasp as the half-chewed Lumpsucker falls into the water and floats downwards. They just stare embarrassingly as the fish floats away, neither one of them brave enough to dip under the water to retrieve it, looking bemused as the small cub looks back at the shore before nestling up against its sibling.

The female, by this point, is quite far out and looks happy enjoying some time to herself, I'm sure she'll stay within earshot of the youngsters though. There's been a subtle change to the sky on the horizon as the distant blue has been mildly invaded by a few darker clouds and the wind has picked up pace. The larger cub leaves the safety of the rock and enters the water, nose first, and merges into the water as its little tail flicks up and disappears. The smaller cub sits upright and peeps in all directions and upwards towards a very vocal passing Tern and a few dotted clouds that have just arrived. She sits there in the full light of the sun and curls up by herself until the first drops of rain fall on her from the small cluster of clouds above. She tentatively sniffs at the water and looks out at her sibling who's just before the shoreline. Loneliness has given in as she dives straight in without grace, causing an Otter shaped splash in her wake. Her head's back up above the water but she looks uncomfortable; she heads slowly towards her sibling and the shore like a slow-moving frog on the top of a pond.

The sun and the light rain have collided, a rainbow has emerged which arches over the bay with a colourful, shattered reflection on the water below. Light and dark blue have drawn a line through the sea like a divide which is where the mother continues to dive for fish. The little one reaches the tide line and pounces all over her sibling as they wrestle and squabble like young animals do. The fighting comes to a halt as they begin preening again.

A Painted Lady butterfly grabs their attention as she floats in front of them with her vibrant orange coat, wings fluttering fast, trying to dodge the heavy drops of rain. They stare at her with curious little eyes and she swerves and sways in their eye line. The two of them give chase to the migrant butterfly but the duo have no chance against her as she lifts high and over the wall and far away up towards the meadow. They settle down once more, heads resting on each other for comfort and gently closing their eyes for a while until their mother returns. They turn away from the sea and feel the warm sun on their backs; they just lay down on the worn-down beach stones as the waves roll into the highest point on the tide line behind them.

The mother's still visible, out in the middle of the bay and seems to be catching many small fish and the occasional Butterfish which she eats out at sea. The cubs blend into their rocky surrounding as their fur starts to turn from dark, cold wet to a warm, soft, dry brown like a well-used teddy bear. These two are the cutest things I've ever seen in the wild and they're oblivious to my presence. The tide is on the turn and the slow, casual waves just about reach their rudder-like tails, just lapping slightly up as far as the Otters. Now they're all dry apart from their soaking tails. The larger cub leaves and heads up further away from the oncoming tide but the little one remains, refusing to move as she's found herself a little haven between the rocks. Now it's just the two of us. She flickers her eyes in the full line of the sun, it feels like she's looking right at me. She blinks up again then closes her eyes tight. The tide isn't hanging about and is pushing in faster now as it reaches her lower back but, still she doesn't move; a big wave almost rolls over her and she just shakes it off and stays put. Her eyes close again and she twitches like she's having a daydream, dreaming of large fish and a warm cosy holt, snuggled up to her sibling and mother. She's not tethered to the rock but seems to get comfort from being wedged in there. Out of the corner of my eye, I see the mother approaching which hasn't gone unnoticed by the larger cub who races out to greet her. The little cub hears the calls and springs into life, leaving her wedged haven and me behind. She's not bringing a meal this time, but the peeps still sound joyous and they bounce all over her until they reach the shore. All three slide away into a small freshwater pool just off the bay and send ripples all around, which moments before, had a mirrored, perfect reflection.

Snipe in the surrounding grasses are sent scuttling and call frantically as they flee the commotion of the Otters. The three Snipe fly just feet above my head. As I remove myself from between a rock and the damp grass and tuck myself into a dip in the bank, I sit straight on a large Thistle which pierces my skin, but I try as hard as possible not to disturb them by making commotion of my own. The three of them are so engrossed with rolling and diving in and out of the water that they pay no attention. The female climbs out and marks her territory on a well-used sprainting spot which is discoloured from the surrounding grass. She looks around and smells the air then rejoins the cubs in the pool. Coming down the slope of the bank is a new Otter, a much bulkier and broader male. The female sits upright as the cubs try and huddle on the lone rock by the edge of the pool. She's watching his every bounding move, squeaks purposely in his direction and gives the small body of water a wide berth, heading down a little Burn into the adjacent bay and out of sight. The female Otter leaves the cubs on the rock and heads in the direction of where the male has headed. I watch on as the young ones bundle together and stay flat to the rock where she left them, like when your mother tells you to stay on the naughty step at the bottom of the stairs not moving until she returns. Just like that, you fidget and move a little with the intention of getting back before she catches you, that's what the cubs are up to, edging into the water and out of the pool then sniffing around the sprainted mound. Suddenly the mother returns and finds them rolling around on the far side of the bank, she calls them over and they turn and run to her like she's been away for days. As they both nuzzle into her, they head back to their bay, the cubs trailing their mother all the way. The female slips right into the incoming tide and the cubs stop still and watch her drift further from them and onto a small island fifty metres or so out. The breeze has died away, and the sun overpowers the last of the dotted clouds leaving the water in a state of reflective calm. The cubs watch on as the female swims around the small island, sticking close to the rocky haven. Finally, after much thought, the larger cub enters the high water and the little one follows swiftly behind as they head out into the bay leaving a trail of swirling ripples behind them as they paddle and dive in unison.

The bay has opened-up in front of them and the high tide has hidden most of the rocks from the surface. Gannets are circling up high, out at sea, looking for an opportunity to dive torpedo-style into the water for fish, their pure white coats with black wing tips are just visible up high. One twist of the wing and a mid-air pirouette and he's in full speed towards the surface, he rips the through calm water like a bullet and he's down almost half a minute before booming back up like a cork, flapping hard to get airborne, similar to a Swan in take-off and then we have lift off. He re-joins the other circling Gannets to continue their search.

Meanwhile the smaller cub is coming ashore with many legs coming out of her mouth. As she cuts through the water, she looks agitated, carrying a large green Shore Crab and is being pursued closely by her brother. She releases the crustacean as soon she feels solid ground and they squabble over it, trying to bite through the hard shell but being wary of the pincers as the Crab tries to find safety in the water but they're not letting their prize catch get away this time. The little cub finds the courage and I can hear the crunches from the rock I'm sat against; they seem to have reached an agreement and both get a fair share of the feast with each one having a little platform like' a mini dinner table a few feet apart. Within minutes the meal has been devoured and only tiny fragments of the feast are left on the rocky table. Looking very satisfied, both cubs rest tightly together; it's hard to work out whose body parts are whose, in the Otter-ball.

An Oystercatcher is walking along the shoreline and hasn't noticed me or the little brown mass of Otter; he looks upright and proud with his pied body and deep red pointed bill. As he approaches, he lets off a loud call and one the Otters rolls over and peeps back at the incoming bird which jumps up, startled, but stands its ground and carries on walking the line he was on, not fazed by the small, potential threat. Usually they go mad at the presence of a predator, or anything that moves within their territory but this plucky Oystercatcher thinks it's his lucky day and just saunters right by and the young Otters barely raise a muscle and just watch him go by, then close their eyes tightly once more.

I haven't seen the female for a while, she must've gone onto the island for a rest of her own. It gives me time to just lay here and stare up at the passing clouds, doing nothing, and the beautiful smell of the sea in the summer is caressing the shoreline and colliding with the flower meadow behind me. The youngsters haven't moved a muscle in a while; the ball of brown fur is only thirty feet in front of me. The time passes by so quickly as Turnstone and Dunlin forage around the Otters as though they are sped up to make a time lapse. The Otters are oblivious to the waders flitting around them as they sleep soundly on the shore. I seem oblivious too as I look down at my hand to see a party of ants have colonised my palm without me noticing. I had got completely lost in staring out to sea with the Otters in the foreground that time had become irrelevant.

A Wren rattles off its loud and distinctive call within earshot of me; he hasn't noticed me laying here in the grass. He calls again with a sharp song from a small rock low to the ground just a few feet away. The noise brings me abruptly back to my near surroundings. I have no idea how long I've been sat by this rock, but it must be hours as the water appears to be heading out again and the rocks that were engulfed are now rising above the surface again. The seaweed is glistening from the low-lying sun which is skirting the horizon and almost refusing to go down. The cubs finally awake from an extremely long nap and are, not so gracefully, walking away from the water in the direction of the mound with the dip on the grassy bank. Meandering up a well-worn path, they leave the retreating tide and low sun behind as they reach the top of the mound. The little duo, sit, staring out in the direction of where their mother is then fall flat to the warm ground. They tangle themselves together again to the point of almost merging into one animal; I can just see the tops of their heads as they sink further into the dip. Their eyes fall shut again, despite only just waking from a long nap.

The mother has left the sea without my noticing and ambles amongst the rocks in the direction of the mound. She stops briefly to mark her territory on a large rock and then carries on until she reaches the flat grass and the base of the mound. The cubs' heads spring up as she clambers up; there's no boisterous greeting for her this time. She slips in between them to join in with the brown furry tangle; it's not long before all of them have their eyes tightly shut against the low sun. The mother lays in the middle with both cubs leaning their head into hers, with the smaller cub flicking her tail over the back of her mother.

I leave them with their mother in the place where I found them when the sun was high. By now the sun's attempting to fall behind the low-lying hill in front of the croft; it'll soon set for the shortest while. I'm joining the sun in departing over the hill and down the dusty track before the fairies come out looking for mischief in the briefest glimpse of summer darkness.

The Forest

The river snakes around the monumental rock that stands tall, seemingly guarding between the edge of the forest and the river.

I leave the river that sits underneath the east side of the overhanging crag and fumble up the Anemone covered slope that meets the loose path, trying to tread carefully between the little delicate white flowers on the uneven bank. A fleeting glimpse of a Jay meets me as I reach the flat of the path, just enough to catch a flash of the soft, dirty pink and white rump as it vanishes high up behind the newly emerged wall of leaves. I stumble across a small clearing in the otherwise thick wood that smells dry and floral, with no sign of flowers on the floor, they must have blown across from the Anemones down the bank. Three Common Lizards with flattened bodies bask on rusty brown, dead bracken, the tiny dinosaur replicas, like me, are making the most of the late afternoon sun.

An early male Nightingale fires off a short, bursting, sweet tune from its impressive repertoire, reminiscent of a Blackbird with a microphone; it lasted just a handful of seconds and now nothing. I sit on a felled, mossy log and wait. A Chiffchaff breaks up my wait with an incessant call as it works its way through the tops of the trees. Just as the two-tone song of the Chiffchaff gets more and more faint, the Nightingale belts out its opening track, again followed by more of his seemingly out of control vocals. He is joined by a backing vocalist in the shape of the tiny Wren, his song is explosive and pierces through the call of the Nightingale, but not for long. The master of the dusk chorus turns up the volume as he rattles off a machine gun style trill that lasts over half a minute; it sounds like he's singing next to my head, yet still I can't see him through the dense thickets of the edge of the clearing. He is making himself well and truly heard though, stealing back all the attention and staying well hidden in the limelight.

He's quiet for a moment, and in that time, I can hear a host of other birds perform their relatively limited range in comparison, but beautiful, nonetheless. He calls again from the scrub with yet another piece of a song that's more subtle to start with but erupts with a glorious Beatles-esque finish to round it off. A second Nightingale has been forced to reply, louder and straight to his quickfire trill. He's calling from behind me so now the Nightingale concert is being played in surround sound in the bracken filled amphitheatre to an audience of one. The two songsters take their turn to outdo the other one, more elongated trills and perfect melodies come from both birds until they end up singing together in a cacophony of warbling noise until they reach the summit of the crescendo and it stops dead. There's nothing to be heard by either bird but the sound of the Chiffchaff, Wren and lonesome Dunnock filter back through; it's time to leave the clearing if I'm to get to the river's edge with time to spare.

It's not long before my next encounter with noise, dominating the moment, as a Peregrine's forceful call echoes hauntingly down and cuts through the forest. She circles just above the trees; she's clearly bothered by something as she nests high up on the crag to defend her territory and her chicks from anything she deems a threat. Through the clear areas of the branches the vague shape of a Raven comes into view and the Falcon calls with even more ferocity. I can see just enough of the sky to see the two birds together, the Falcon diving at ridiculous speeds at the large, dark corvid, screaming every time she stoops towards the Raven who is doing his best to avoid the agile Falcon. He drops as quickly as possible into the wood, knowing the Peregrine won't be venturing under the tree line. He aims three powerful croaks back up to the Falcon who's still calling furiously as she drifts away. Sharing a territory with a Peregrine brings its own set of problems but this dispute is over for now.

This five-minute walk has taken me over half an hour now. I jump off the main path and onto a slippery bank that has a dried-up stream that slopes through the thin trees, giving me something to follow as it'll lead me to the river at the bottom. The smell of Wild Garlic drifts through the wood on a warm breeze; there's no sight of the heavily scented plant in my view but I know there are some patches near the riverbank - I'm nearly there.

As the day passes a certain point, the calls from birds start to hum through the forest, a Robin sings in my face from an overhanging tree and follows me down the empty stream, flying a few feet in front of me every time and chirping happily away from any platform he can land his tiny legs on. He's interrupted by the loud drumming sound of a Woodpecker letting any others of its kind know that this is his territory. He's just visible midway up an old Beech tree which is the only tree in view not plastered in fresh leaf cover. With his body pressed up against the pale bark he continues to hammer into its side, taking short breaks in between to reset his position. He tilts his head downwards and sees me peering up at him; he takes less than one second to work me out before flapping, quickly off the old Beech, a frantic blur of black, white and red seep into green with a bouncy-type flight and he's gone.

I can make out the flow of the river through the last line of trees. The sight of the west river is welcoming, the wonderous sound of flowing water over rounded rocks is pulling me in its direction. For the briefest moment, I've filtered out bird song and all other sounds of the wood, as all I can hear is the sound of the river below me. The dry stream that's my path becomes ever steeper as I near the end, spindly trees flank the stream and are very useful handholding devices as I scramble backwards down the slope. A small forest of Ferns cling to the steep-sided rock and greets me near the bottom. A Blackbird is screeching in full-throttled alarm just to my left. He draws my attention to a figure sitting amongst the foliage just off the trunk of the Oak thirty-ish feet away; it's almost at the same eye-line as me. On slightly closer inspection, I can make out the shape of an Owl as he breaks the usual silhouette of Ivy that's hugging close to the trunk, chestnut brown washes down between the pale strokes. The many different shades of brown drape and drip down his chest and dark streaks line up in perfect symmetry around his slumped, sleepy face and meet almost heart-shaped above the eyes. His eyes are firmly shut, his feet are covered in what looks like hand-knitted woollen cloth that just about covers as far as its talons that are grasping tightly around the thin branch amongst the Ivy. It's the first time I've ever had a view of a still Tawny Owl and he's captivating, almost perfect. I edge carefully and as quietly as possible but step unknowingly on a twig that crunches too loudly for the Owl and his big, black eyes open wide and stare me down. He doesn't need a second glance, he spreads his wings to the tips and tumbles out of the Ivy, arcing in the opposite direction from me and vanishes in a swirl of tawny brown towards where the sunlight is leaking through the trees.

I carry on my journey and hop onto the gritty path that runs parallel to the river, the bone-dry track cuts in and out of the wood beside the river as birds start to fill the late May day with song starting with the ever-present Robin who seems to be following me as there's one singing melodically away every fifty metres or so. The Robins are joined by Dunnocks and a couple of Great Tits that shout out the same repetitive tune over, and over again, to the point of getting annoyingly stuck in my head. Thankfully, the dry, laughing call from a Magpie stops most of the birds singing, including the Great Tits, if only for a moment until the mainly pied corvid has flown across to the other side of the river and the singing can resume.

For weeks I've been walking past this point and today's the day, I'm going to settle down and wait in the hope of seeing two great Mustelids. On the wooded bank is a very established Badger Sett that overlooks the riverside where a shallow, stony beach has clear Otter tracks pressed firmly into the spit of grainy sand. At the end of the beach is a slightly raised patch of bright, tufted grass. Spraints have been piling up on top of the small mound and some are so fresh, like I've missed an Otter by minutes. The many holes of the Badger Sett are dotted around with the main entrances at the steep point in the middle, with nettles and a few Wood Anemones for company. Tracks are woven forcefully through a carpet of Bluebells at the flatter base of the bank; the bells are turning over to rest for the night after a long day of undisturbed, early summer sunshine. Piles of Badger poo fill a deeply dug hole; it should smell sweet, but a Fox has left its own scat next to the Badgers' toilet and its pungent smell dominates. Even an Otter has rudely marked his territory on top of the Badger latrine.

Stepping away from the mammals at a convenient point and taking myself a little distance away, I sit in front of an Ivy-covered stump. My backdrop will hide my silhouette and I'll hopefully go unseen and let the forest reset itself, giving me more chance of seeing the secretive and sensitive animals. I'm helped in my aim to go unnoticed massively by the overpowering smell of Wild Garlic that wafts through, masking my scent as I sit downwind of the Sett and the river. Sitting still and patiently waiting brings things that would otherwise not be seen, such as a Nuthatch that climbs the side of an Oak that overhangs the river to my left; he climbs the trunk like he's on rails, his delicate peach front and light grey back, with a hint of a mask around its head, stick out against the dark-etched brown bark. A late Bumblebee clambers around a lone, deep pink Thistle flower, trying desperately to cling on to its delicate petals; the orangey-red buff tip is in complete contrast to its bulky black body and a faint pale ribbon that wraps around its base. A Ladybird draws my attention as it climbs up the stem and carefully crawls through the layers of soft hair and around the unforgiving spines that guard the flower; his bright red, armoured shell is dotted with tiny black spots, with two white marks on a small head of black. He ambles up to where the Bee is busy preparing for lift off. The Bumblebee hovers briefly before giving up and falling sharply before resting on the flower again, she tries again. I can hear her tiny wings humming as she becomes airborne and flies a short distance and settles in the thick patch of Bracken. The Ladybird circles the flower head before settling in the corner of a comfy, pink flower bed.

Across the river, a Song Thrush is bellowing down from the top of a golden Willow as a Blackcap sings between the long, draping leaves that fall all the way to touch the surface of the water. Every bird seems to have suddenly come out of the shadows to join in for the chorus at dusk. The forest is alive with sound as Chaffinch, Goldfinch and the cheerful Blue Tit all add their voices to the noise. A calling Buzzard just above the tree line brings the chorus to an abrupt end.

The late, spring sun is glaring at me through the trees, the light is catching the tips of the
Bluebells and is casting a peaceful, late light, on the unfolded Bracken leaves that will be hidden behind the bank soon as it creeps slowly up the Sett. A passing Kingfisher brings my attention back to the river as he flies low, over the river calling

with three, sharp peeps, before disappearing, leaving a flash of blurring blue behind. Mayflies are also making the most of their one-day life as they dance and skim, seemingly out of control, just above the surface of the water. The last of the sunlight shimmers as it passes through their wings and dapples the ripples of water in gold. The river makes a giggling sound as it's tickled by the rocks that have been left behind as the water level has dropped from the lack of recent rainfall. The slightest of milky mists is forming, almost at the exact moment the sun dips behind the darkened far bank.

Without warning there's a short, sharp bursting squeak coming from a small patch of Nettles up to my right, I can't see any movement around the main entrances except for a tiny Wren who is working her way, mouse-like, through the bedded Bluebells. The high-pitched call continues as I strain my neck to get a different angle without moving too much. Lime green stinging Nettle leaves move unnaturally just twenty feet away and I stay as still as my patience allows as they more than partially obscure an entrance I hadn't even seen. I've been watching the main holes, the ones with the freshly dug soil lying below them and strewn pieces of old bedding grasses sitting above. Through the patch of troublesome Nettles, a nose appears, a broad, black nose, twitching away as it pushes back the overgrown plant, two black stripes streak down its face and rest on a glorious white head. He looks agitated and unwilling to bring himself fully out of the protective cover. His nose and ears are working overtime to check the air for any unwanted dangers. He sniffs left, right, up, down and then left again before grunting grumpily upwards before repeating that process another three times; he shuffles himself backwards and he's gone. Two minutes he spent listening and tasting his surroundings before vanishing and leaving the area of the Sett. With an empty feeling, it felt like a one-off show was about to start but was abandoned early as the star had to cancel, last minute. Maybe he caught my scent, or something didn't quite feel right; Badgers are highly sensitive and never compromise the safety of their clan if there's even the slightest of doubts and I, on this occasion, must've been that doubt. I gaze back down in the direction of the grainy beach as a Grey Wagtail works the edges, its tail is bobbing constantly as it ambles around the water line, plucking as many tiny insects off the rocks before darkness sets in.

The show that I thought was cancelled has got the go ahead as a Badger appears from the furthest hole, no warning, no air-sniffing, just straight into the main bare patch, away from the Bluebell tracks and sitting boldly out in the open; he's trying desperately to scratch the place that seems impossible to reach. Two smaller Badgers of black, white and fluffy grey bounce out like they're on a trampoline; they're noticeably smaller than the scratching male and are using all their youthful exuberance to chase each other's tails around in playful circles. The newly emerged cubs make a beeline for the male, like two charging Rhinos. Just before any collision with the uninterested male, they part, either side of him, and clatter together into a ball of grey that smatters into the purple-tinged, blue and green flowers that won't stay carpeted with these two around. Whilst the two boisterous youngsters are frolicking around at the far edges, another three Badgers have emerged and join the male in the middle. My Ivy stump and the direction of the garlic-infused breeze is concealing my presence, for now, as I watch on as the six Badgers scratch, preen, bounce and run around the Sett.

Every so often, I glance to the river in the hope of seeing v-shaped ripples, swirling water or an Otter standing on the stony beach. I look back as one of the cubs is tumbling through the Nettles and getting ever closer to me. He stops and lazily sniffs the air in my direction before sitting upright. He looks like his little black eyes are staring straight at me with just a casual glint in them from the fading light. I hold my breath and count slowly to ten in my head, thankfully, he looks down at his fluffy chest and paws away with his long claws across his belly. The other Badgers congregate together behind the largest hole and continue to nibble and scratch away at their fur. An adult Badger helps the cub by pawing the base of the tail of the youngster, in the place he just can't reach; it's a gentle touch that only his mother can give him, and he seems to enjoy the moment. The cub sticks close to its mother, nuzzling at her face and trying to force his way under her; she's not having any of it and he's way too big to fit underneath her. The other cub remains in front of me, he looks dazed as he stares upwards at the darkening silhouettes of the branches, he turns to seemingly face me again, his nose twitching inquisitively and sniffs at me again. He stood still for a moment before turning away at speed, he charges back towards his clan who are still busy cleaning and scratching themselves. I thought he was running off to let them know of my presence, but he just settles tightly beside his mother and brother. They'll soon be heading off to forage into the night for the few amounts of darkness hours this time of year allows.

A pitter, patter, squeaky call is coming from the bank of the river, the Grey Wagtail flies away hastily from the edge of the beach, a fluttering mix of soft, slate grey and sulphur yellow, goes over my head and up into the woods; he's left the grainy beach behind, empty. Around the far edge the shallow water pulses, and a flash of watery brown fur flicks above the surface, it's tail thrashes uncontrollably about and is the only thing visible for a split second before disappearing under the water. The river resumes its soft flow to almost stillness.

The far end of the bank is partially obscured by an overhanging branch and I try to move slightly for a better angle without disturbing the Badgers who are still scratching and squabbling about at the main open patch of the Sett. I can't see any movement around the beach or anywhere across the river and the only sound is coming from the Song Thrush, the only remaining bird singing high up in the willow. I arch my head as far as it'll reach around the branch but there's nothing further down river either, nothing breaking the surface or pushing against the current. The Otter looks like it's past the small amount of river in my view, giving me a fleeting glimpse of his back and a flick of its dark, brown tail and stealthily left unseen. I turn back to the Badgers who look like they're readying themselves to head off on a foraging trip; the mother looks like she's barking orders at the youngsters who look set to miss out on tonight's trip and have to settle for a night in at the Sett instead. Just as I thought, the adults head across the far bank one by one, and in a line. One of the cubs chases its mother and nips at her matted tail; she snarls at her offspring and heads through a tunnelled hole in a Bramble bush leaving the cub to scratch his belly for a moment before returning to the Sett and his waiting sibling who just stayed put.

It won't be long until they're mature enough to be taken on the evening forays.

Then, skulking low to the water at the far side, is the return of the Otter, its distinctive shape is cutting across the water. The slightly wavering v shape is rippled as it passes the middle of the quickest flow near the larger rocks. The Otter surges out of the river leaving the water to fall off its back, his tail draped in the water. He settles on the edge of the grainy reef and scratches frantically into the cold, coloured sand, pawing at it like there's something there. He rolls over onto his back and rubs his coat against the scratch marks. He sits still for the first time, time enough for me to get a good look at him. He's got an old story-filled face with a few nicks around his ears and a half moon scar through his soft, pink nose. As he sniffs the air which is starting to have a crispness to it as the cold starts to draw in with a lingering hint of garlic, he looks up and down the river but never behind him at the bank. He looks unsure as to which way to go and I'm not sure which direction he came from. He stretches out his back legs and ruffles his pelt before slipping quietly into the water. The remaining Badgers mosey back towards the main entrance of the Sett, sit briefly above it for one last scratch before ambling side by side and slink down the hole and out of sight. This is my chance to remove myself from the Ivy stump, skidding down the slope trying to draw as little attention to myself as possible, but every broken twig magnifies the sound twice-over in the almost soundless evening.

Hopefully, the Otter hasn't wandered too far up stream; he hasn't got far at all as his serpentine movements through the dead-centre of the river make him easy to pick out. The river is painted with deep, blue hues. As I follow the Otter up against the flow of the water, he meanders from side to side, only diving to get ahead of himself and not particularly to forage. The Otter makes a beeline for the near bank and pulls himself up onto a fallen, semi-aquatic branch, and rests his head on the dampened bark. His long whiskers drip inky-coloured water down onto the surface as he holds his stare at a dark shape, loosely hidden behind the base of a tree; he's refusing to turn away until he figures out what it is or if it moves. His head slumps even further down until it's almost flat with the branch, his nose sniffs towards me, and in that split second, he spins off the branch and plunges back into the water hurriedly. He has picked up on the slightest scent from me, a scent the Badgers had missed, or been more familiar with. I wait against the base of the tree for a minute before setting off up-river again.

Clouds begin to form, high above the river, for what feels like the first time today - I'm sure there were a few, cloudy outbreaks, at the start of the afternoon. Thin shards cut across the clear canvased sky, invading the empty space, like shouting out loudly in a silent room.

The path leaves the river at this point before cutting back under an arch of branches and meeting a natural cascade; an elongated waterfall where the river closes into its narrow point, sloped rocks act as a natural gate for the water to fall through. Another high-pitched sound comes from the darkness near the top; it's the Otter again. Crouching down and silhouetted against a backdrop of a cloudless reflective sky, he peeps again before marking his territory in the most obvious of prominent places. His scent will drift far down the river from that high point and catch a ride on the river's air stream. He slides into the almost stagnant water that's congregated before the rocks and drifts upstream, occasionally, erratically, surfacing, shattering the still. He's going at some pace and it's hard to keep track of him in the ever, darkening sky. The first Tawny Owl calls sharply to fill the silence the songbirds have left behind; it's coming from the woods where I came from and could be the beautiful bird from earlier.

The twilight blue river is evenly split down the middle into darkness and light from the overbearing, shadowy bank with reflections from a dwindling, deeply clouded scarred sky. Darkness and light seem to sum up the last few hours perfectly.

The lone male Otter continues his way but now he's slowed right down, he twists himself around as he forages under a mass of roots that are submerged in the water. For a few minutes he swirls, only partially revealing himself above the water and emerges with what looks like a small Eel, takes it in his mouth to a spit of pebbles on the far side of the river from me, drops it on the flat and tries to adjust the squirming creature within his paws. There's a slither of silvery light on the body of the snakelike fish which is also streaking down the wet fur of the Otter. The Eel tries every which way to escape the clutches of the Otter, he almost makes it back into the sanctuary of the water before the Otter pounces on him again - there's no escape this time as the Otter tears into the slippery elongated fish; the crunching sound is easy to hear across the quiet of the river. He makes short work of his evening's catch as he takes a timeout to shake vigorously before nibbling at his front feet.

The Otter stops, frozen still for a moment, stares towards the far bank where I'm crouched in a patch of Nettles that I'd not realised were sharply stinging my left hand. I'd not noticed the irritating tiny barbs when the Otter was feeding but, now he's glaring intensely in my direction, it's all I can think about. I want to scratch the stings so much but cannot move until he does; like him I'm trying to remain motionless, playing a game in a complex staring competition and I'm not even sure he can see me at all. A minute passes by; it feels like an excruciating sixty second attack on my wrist and the back of my hand but I'm unable to move. Thankfully he breaks from his frozen state, springs up with a burst of erratic energy and bounds towards the river's edge, entering the shallow water with a graceful fluidity; I've never been more relieved to see an Otter leave than that. I plunge my hand in the cold water of the river to relieve a little of the irritation, if only for a few seconds.

The clouds are getting louder and louder as they force their way in across the sky, the dying embers are barely lighting anything that's not reflective. It'll soon be too dark for the moon is only a few days old and not strong enough to cast any more than a trickle of light over the river and the forest.

I walk up onto an old brick bridge and stare at the river's edges in the hope of one last glimpse from the enigmatic Otter, but the river is running in slow motion and nothing's disturbing it's flow. The Otter is nowhere to be seen up the barrel of the river for as far as I can see in the fading light. A pair of regal-looking Swans float across the river with heads held high leaving dark ripples behind as they push and glide effortlessly through the river. Suddenly, their tranquil swimming stops as they span their wings out fully, hissing loudly. The Otter appears just to their left but is only passing by; the Swans alter their route and paddle furiously in his direction, but he's slipped under the surface as they continue hissing at the empty water where he was. He emerges well away from where he dived, leaving the swans to paddle around in angry circles. He's just a distant black shape, given away by his distinctive v shape which is fading away in the water. He enters a dark patch of river, blackened by the thick, tall trees that line either slope; his silhouette is engulfed by it and I'll not see the Otter again tonight.

At the exact moment of the Otter's disappearance, a Fox barks out from beyond the far-side trees, near the crescent moon-shaped field, its call cuts right through me; it's both terrifying and comforting at the same time, making me feel that I'm not alone. Another Owl calls out from deep within the forest and it's time for me to leave.

The path has become blocked with twisted shadows from the trees that reach out across my way. Short, muffled noises are coming out of the bank up to my right; it's the delicate sounds of scraping leaf litter from emerging rodents as they scurry about in the undergrowth. A late flock of Rooks fall out of the trees and croak as they fly around in a circle to land high up in the tree from where I'd disturbed them. The river again comes into view as I strain my eyes and gather as much natural light as possible. Little rings of dark grey, pencil sketch patterns, are etched on the middle of the river and are surrounded almost entirely by black, still water. There's more light if I turn around to face the point where the sun went down, but it's just a small gathering of paler, blue light in the dark canvas of sky.

The Fox lets out another eerie screech once more and well and truly signals the start of the night for the forest.

The Rainbow Otters

The sky is overcast with the smell of rain in the air as I head up onto the narrow track that guides its way through the old wood, Moss soaks the rocky walls on either side. The gap in the old Oaks at the top of the twisted track reveal a glimpse of the shore below. The wings of a Jay flash through the parting of the Birch that shines like iridescent oil spilt on a rainy road. A Buzzard circles and cries out just above the top of the wood and glides out of my sight. The trees become sparse as I'm nearing the end of the track and the sea is becoming more and more visible, turning from trees and green to rocks and blue; it's like opening the curtains to another world. An Oystercatcher is calling with panic from bay to bay, and in contrast, the sweetly spoken Wren sings with a gentle yet forceful song. Thousands of broken shells crack under foot as I walk the lonesome tideline. The sky is showing signs of breaking and the smell of the coast is unforgettable, mixed with all the sounds, it's a place that makes me feel more alive. The waves are pulsing like a hardened heartbeat as a Sandpiper walks the shore like a clockwork toy and makes its nest like a tiny empire built out of pebbled sand.

I skate on the slippery rocks and peer into the small pools left behind by the tide. Brittle Star and Cushion Starfish are seeking refuge under the rocks in the shallows; a beautiful mosaic of cold purple and almost lime green seaweed sit on the edges, as empty cockles and abandoned shells line the floor of the pool. Tiny Green Shore Crabs jostle for the best rocks, cherry tomato Anemones cling to the side with fingers stretched out, Microscopic Shrimp follow each other like water sheep; one massive ecosystem in a two-foot rock pool, it's other worldly ripples and reflections like abstract works of art from sky to sea.

The stone arms of the old pier are sheltering the bay from the ever-increasing wind that's still in the bay, clogged with a mix of bright yellow and dark brown seaweed. A few scattered rocks stick just above the water with a small army of the famous west highland Midge having a briefing before going into battle. In the distance a handful of Gannets are circling below the low cloud and scanning the sea for a target. It would be difficult to spot anything in the sea except from within the sheltered bay. A pair of Eider drift away from the calm of the bay and out to sea as I get ever nearer. There are many white horses on the waves, and they are imitating rising Dolphins as I try harder to focus on the water between the waves. The sun and tide turn in sync and the mood changes; suddenly the calls have changed, and the water is heading for the slack. The tiny Sandpiper leaves behind a high-pitched whistle as it heads from the prominent rock in the bay. The Oystercatcher wheels away in alarmed panic, leaving its call to echo around the tiny bay.

An Otter ambles from some dead Oaks sloping to the shore and slips into the clear water in one, sleek motion. She's lost under the water as she's transforming her coat into a beautiful wetsuit. She comes up a few metres further out and drifts through the shore rocks, past a cloud of Midges, dives with one perfect action, arched and with a flick of her tail into another world below the surface. I count the seconds as I imagine what it must be like in the meadow of the seaweed and shimmering rocks, and then she's up again. She's bringing up small fish and eating them on the go, crunching her way through them at speed.

The clouds have let go of the rain they were holding tightly within them so I retreat to sit under the overhang of one of the Oaks with a rock in front of me, between the pier and the slope. Suddenly the Otter's attention is grabbed by a short, sharp whistle, coming towards the old pier. She immediately returns the call, instantly recognisable to her as another Otter within her territory. The intruder sees her and heads straight towards her without a dive, paddles at speed with all four legs working hard and a tail that's almost wagging as he goes. They meet in the middle of the bay and instead of squabbling over residence rights, their greeting is joyous and touching. They roll above and below the surface for a few minutes and it's clear this is her cub. The rain has hardened but it hasn't stopped the Midges from pestering my face as I watch the two Otters swim around together in the bay, separating midway in the bay as the mother carries on foraging for food on the ever-changing tide. The cub keeps a watchful eye for his mother as he occasionally comes up at different times and calls out frantically until she surfaces and he's content once more. The cub heads in the direction of the huge rock I'm hidden behind; just visible are two eyes, a flat head and a bunch of whiskers sifting through the jungle maze of kelp. He's coming onto shore with a small Butterfish, he clambers onto the rock just before the one I'm wedged behind. Tiny water droplets fly off the fur and sparkle in the light after a vigorous shake and he starts to feed on his well-earned prize, he's lined up beautifully with the distant breaking clouds and is unaware of my existence. Watching something behave so naturally and without caution is a joy and I feel calm in my surroundings.

The sun has managed to pierce a hole in the clouds behind me, shard after shard shatter through and throw their spotlights on the sea where the mother Otter continues to dive for food. I can see every movement and hear every sound coming from the young Otter in front of me, paws still tightly grasped around the fish, like he'll never eat again. He finishes, and with one last shake of his coat, he slips back into the water and heads off, on the surface, in the direction of his mother who's been busy catching small fish herself. The sun relentlessly batters down the wall of cloud as the rain in front of me sweeps across the bay. I'm still relatively sheltered from the rain but there's no protection from the ferocious Midges. The two Otters embrace again in the calmest part of the bay. The rays of light collide with the sweeping rain to produce the start of a rainbow above the Bracken-covered peninsula. The Otters seem in no hurry and carry on playing and diving through the water without any real purpose or seemingly heading in any particular direction.

The clouds above the hill behind me open-up and allow more light to flow through, the rainbow instantly becomes more vivid as blue greets violet at the bottom as red merges into yellow, with green hues at the top, the colours trickling over the waves and into the reflective calm where the Otters are still twisting and turning through the water. A party of Gannets become silhouetted as they pass in front of the mass of distant colour. The blue hues at the bottom of the rainbow almost touch the tops of the white horses out at sea where the flock of Eider surf the larger waves. The two Otters float together at the bottom of the rainbow as the tide gradually rises. The Otters look drawn onto a picture-perfect canvas as they begin to change gear and head past the pier.

The colourful bow disappears fully from sight as the clouds have closed in and blocked the sun. The Oystercatcher returns to the sheltered bay with the Sandpiper lagging just behind. The young Otter tailgates its mother as they drift on the current around the bay and out of sight behind a sloping sea crag.

After many attempts, the full attack begins. I'm swarmed by tiny little flying assassins armed to cause maximum pain from minimum contact. As they advance, it's time for me to retreat with the fading light and leave the Midges and the Otters behind.

A Glorious Summers Marsh

The sun's taking an eternity to drop and just sits there, seemingly motionless, refusing to fall as we pass the mid-afternoon point. The single Reed stem sways in a fluid motion with the light summer breeze until it joins the others and the mass of stems all move in unison like waves on an incoming tide.

The deep-throated booming call from a male Bittern reverberates over the tops of the Reeds. Damsel and Dragonflies are busy recreating scenes from fighter jet combat and are dominating the sky. A male Emperor Dragonfly comes into land on a piece of old wood sticking out of the shallow, still water, its iridescent blue is a beautiful and obvious contrast to the burnt yellow backdrop of the Reeds. He's making the most of the warmth in this season and soaking up as much of it as he can; his time will soon come to an end but for now he owns the small realm around him and will fight to protect it.

Everything seems so busy right now as the mass of Swallows are joined by House and Sand Martins whirling in from all angles over the tops of the Reeds. These aerial acrobats are twisting and spiralling in search of any flying insects which all seem to be out right now. The flock spins away in a mass of panic as a Hobby comes into view where the water meets the wood at the far edge. The long winged visiting Falcon isn't given a warm welcome or has any intentions of a pleasant greeting of his own as he sweeps his wings back, reaching past the tip of his tail, and, using the sun behind him he ambushes a break away flock of Swallows. The flock breaks away and he turns his fully focused attention to the single Swallow twisting and flapping as fast as its tiny wings will allow him. They both fly higher with the pursuer matching his every erratic move until the Hobby fans his wings and almost stops mid-flight and the Swallow is safe for another day. The Falcon descends back down and glides just above the water's surface until he's out of sight at the far end of the marsh. I've been waiting and watching here for a few hours now just seeing how all these scenes unfold.

There's a raft of wildfowl out on the open water, Ducks and Geese paddle around together in seemingly endless, elongated circles, whilst Grebes and Cormorants dive between a couple of small islands near the middle. A pair of Swans are almost touching as they glide across the water with five, light grey Signets, trailing slightly behind in perfect formation. The male stretches his neck forward and breaks from the formation, he opens his beak and hisses aggressively towards the seemingly empty water with just a lone Coot in the space he's heading, pushing the water behind him as he gathers pace. The Coot looks alarmed and flies away from the approaching Swan who's still hissing in the small area of water he's now alone in; he's clearly sensed there's something he needs to protect his mate and young from. He swims furiously around in small circles creating a mini wave system until the head of an Otter pops up behind him only a few metres away. The Otter submerges before the Swan has seen her and continues circling her endlessly. She again surfaces but this time it's straight in front of the Swan who beats his wings angrily down onto the water, making as much of a commotion as possible. The Otter just stares at the Swan and dives again like it's a game, leaving the swan raging on the surface and having no idea where the little Otter will emerge next. The Otter again bounces up in front of the swan who is clearly at boiling point and hisses in the face of the Otter who responds by making snorting sounds straight back at the swan who arches his neck back and, like a snake, strikes forward at the Otter who dives before the Swan's beak can reach her; it looks like much more of an enjoyable game to the Otter than the Swan. This time the Otter appears further away and carries on her routine leaving the Swan to hiss at the Otter from a little further away. Eventually the male Swan turns away and heads back to his family and back into the formation; he's essentially done his job of keeping threats to his family away even if it didn't really pose much of a threat.

The Otter heads in a line towards a small, flooded bay with a few spindly trees. She wades out onto the soft mud and leaves her footprints behind to join the mass of mainly Duck, Goose and Swan prints already there and settles just out of sight, behind the rushes and the thin trees. I can just make out the brown fur behind the stems, but it looks bigger than it did. I catch more of a glimpse as a nose pokes out at the same time as another little nose pops out on the other side. At least two Otters are crouched behind the curtain of rushes. There's a breakout of peeping calls coming from the bay as a third Otter comes around the other side, through the water carrying what looks like an Eel and lands on the mud. The two Otters break out of the rushes and excitedly bounce all over the approaching Otter who I can only imagine, by their reaction, is the mother of the two as she's a little bigger than them. One of the youngsters grabs the Eel out of the female's grasp and heads quickly for the water's edge. Before he takes his first bite, the other cub leaps onto his head and the Eel squirms away nearer the water; they both scramble for it and slide through the squelchy mud and splash into the shallow water but the Eel has got away. They both look a little lost and curiously stare into the murky water to where the Eel has disappeared but there's no movement.

The mother grooms herself a little further away paying no attention to the cubs losing her catch. The cubs sit together at the water's edge still a bit confused at what's just happened. The mother heads over to them and slips into the water, glances back with a single sharp peep and the cubs fall into line and paddle quickly to catch up to her. As soon as they reach her, she dives under and the cubs quickly do the same; they are out of sight for over half a minute before all surfacing together near the edge of the Marsh and heading closer to me. They meander through short grasses in the low water as Damselflies fly up and fill the area above the surface with their oily, blue wings shimmering as they flicker around in the translucent light. They are heading for a small island that's thick with Reeds and banked with soft mud. Not far out in front of me, the mother Otter leads the cubs through the thick of the Reeds and within seconds they've vanished. If you hadn't seen them go in, you'd never believe there were three Otters curled up in there.

Twenty minutes pass by, and despite squinting at the reeds, I can only just about make out the slightest part of brown fur. Then the female, in an unusually clumsy fashion, bends back the Reeds and saunters through leaving a few gaps to just about see through. She heads around the back of the small island and quickly disappears under the water and doesn't emerge anywhere in sight. I think she was trying to go unnoticed to leave her cubs as safe as possible and draw little or no attention to them. The slight gaps she's left behind have allowed me to just about make out the cubs in the thick nest of mainly trampled Reed stems and a few dead leaves.

Minutes after her departure there's movement amongst the middle of the Reeds as the two Otters begin to fidget and become restless. The larger cub peeks his eyes out boldly through the Reeds as he looks inquisitively down at the water which reflects the passing summery clouds above. His nose twitches as the Reeds brush against it as they sway back and forth from the gentle, warm breeze. The little Otter sits partially in view for a few minutes just staring at the water and up at the occasional passing small and noisy flock of Jackdaw before retreating into the thick of the Reeds and slumping down beside its sibling. Then it's all still and quiet again as they await their mother's return and are only visible when the wind blows through the Reeds and opens them up which makes a quiet whistling sound.

A Kingfisher, dressed in the brightest blue and burnt orange coat lands unannounced on the purple tinged flowering Reeds and peeps unceremoniously down towards the dozing Otters, a little way to his left. He clearly seems annoyed by their presence and carries on peeping at them, then flies a little closer to them; his call turns into more of a high-pitched shrill of an alarm as his posture changes and he looks threatening as he arrows his jet black beak downwards. The two little Otters burst through the stems to see what's making all that noise and disturbing their late afternoon nap. They stare up at the blue bird sitting above them on the flowering Reed that's continuously shouting at them. They huddle together as the smaller one tries to climb over the top of her brother's head for a closer look but falls off and onto the soft mud. They look bemused by the sound which isn't that dissimilar to their own call. One of the youngsters lets off his own peep back at the Kingfisher and that's enough for him as he leaves the Reed and flies low over water, almost skimming the surface as he goes but continuing to call out. I'm sure he's got young of his own nearby and sees the Otters as a threat and that's why he was so alarmed.

The two Otter sniff around the mud at the water's edge as a Heron calls loudly like a yelping dog as it passes low over the small island, with his head tucked in against its stiff wings and legs dangling down like it's coming into land. His flyby is watched intently by the Otters who turn their heads as the fighter jet Grey Heron comes into land on the inlet with spindly trees where the Otters came from earlier. The cubs perk up as they hear the popcorn machine gun sound from the bearded reedlings that ping out through the Reeds. They sound close but are a hard bird to see, especially in the summer when the Reeds are this thick. The sound gets faint as they've passed by without being seen.

It's been over an hour since the female Otter left and the cubs are getting more and more agitated and have taken up the sport of chase the Damselfly of which there's only going to be one winner as the small insects just fly away from the approaching Otters, and scraping at the mud which looks repetitive - they soon lose interest in that too. The smaller cub peers back into the reeds and disappears once more into the makeshift hidden holt. The other cub is still keen on chasing Damselflies but as soon as they settle, they launch off again and out of the reach of the frustrated but playful Otter. He's soon tired of that game too and joins his sibling within the Reeds and the Damselflies settle on the warm mud on the edges.

More time goes by without any movement and still there's no return of the female who's left them for quite a while. Suddenly, there's panic as the raft of wildfowl call alarmingly and as one takes to the sky, a Marsh Harrier floats through the channels and towards the open water. A Moorhen and a couple of Coots run on the water, leaving a bubbly trail behind as they whirl out of the path of the approaching predator. He quarters the largest part of the Reedbed before dropping suddenly into the Reeds at the far end of the Marsh as Snipe fly out in all directions in the place where he fell. He doesn't reappear and normal service resumes out on the water as the Ducks and Geese return. There was no movement from the cubs and hasn't been for a while as the day moves into its last quarter of light.

The pig-like squeal from the elusive Water Rail deep within the Reeds, and the sudden croaky quacks from a pair of Mallards, alerts me to the right where there's swirly movement in the water, around the edges. A glimpse of a tail flicking through, churning, turning the water murky and then the head of the returning female pops up amongst the Yellow Flag Iris and Lily pads looking like a creature rising-up from the deep. Her eyes peer around, keeping herself completely still before submerging, not unlike the way an Alligator does in the everglades. For a few minutes there's no sign of her but I'm sure she came up somewhere un-noticed so I scan around.

A lone Snipe screeches out from the edge of the Reeds as the Otter comes out of the water and onto the mud as she slips through the side of the Reeds where her offspring have been sleeping. They hadn't noticed her approach but the peeping calls sound excited with a happiness to the high-pitched noise. All three of them come storming through and onto the flat; the youngsters are desperately trying to get close to their mother as they roll over and under her until she's forced to stop by her boisterous cubs. They both nuzzle their faces furiously against hers; she's only been back a few minutes and already she looks like she should've been away a little longer; she shakes her head and raises up her neck which gets them both off. She takes to the water again and is instantly joined by the one splashing youngster as the smaller one seems reluctant to leave the safety of the small island. The mother and the bigger cub swim above the water, and despite elongated peeps from the remaining cub, she finally gets the message and plunges into the water; she paddles as fast as her little front and back legs will allow until she's within touching distance of them.

The sun sits just above the old Oak wood and blinds the water out in the middle to where they are heading. The three leave v lines behind as they head through the brightest part of the marsh; the Ducks and Geese are once again parting as the Otters go past.

In complete synchronicity, they dive and leave very little splash behind as they go, but just enough to shatter the surface and throw up a few sparkled droplets into the air. They appear at the far side of the Marsh, near the base of one of the old Oak woods like it's been here well before this area was flooded when it was part of the great forest. Led by their mother, they head up onto the large, tangled web of roots, with the smaller cub needing a bit of teasing out of the water, but she joins them. After a brief stop for a shake-down and a stretch, they head under the largest root and they are gone, out of sight after their exploits out on the Marsh. Cormorants sit high above the roots at the top of the old Oak like Jurassic figurines, dipped in tar, with their wings drooped down to receive the full exposure of the sun on their backs to dry themselves.

I leave the water's edge and weave through the loose path that cuts through the Reeds towards the wood. I'm clear of the Reeds and behind me I can still hear the calls from gaggling Geese and the sweet twittering from the mass of Swallows. I make my way up a slender track which is straddled by tall grasses and overgrown nettles that guard the mixed wood of mainly Black Poplar trees. Butterflies float furiously from the track as I disturb them from bathing in the last of the dipping sun as many more fly in and out of the thin wood; two White Admirals fight over territory rights and encircle each other from low down until they pass the canopy and high up into the deep, blue haze of the sky.

A Red Admiral sits a few feet away on a Nettle leaf and spreads its wings and flattens its body to get the most out of the remaining sun, its mostly black body turning an almost ruddy brown with the fore wings dripping red, painted patterns with a splash of white on the edges; he doesn't mind my presence, so long as I don't cast him in shadow. So, I edge slighter closer until my face is within a foot of his, close enough to see the powdery flecks that make up his colours and pattern, his body and his twitchy, long antenna. Enough is enough as he folds back his wings to change into his pure black jacket, and with a blink of an eye, he's airborne and heading in the direction of a slightly larger Peacock butterfly who's drifting effortlessly across his path.

The Poplar trees that almost dominate the right side of the track seem to sing as the summer wind tickles through the leaves and a chorus of Grasshoppers, like a wind section of an orchestra, join in with the soundtrack of the summer wood as a Wren provides yet another beautiful solo performance.

Up ahead a Roe Deer saunters casually out of the wood and onto the path; he stops to looks both ways up and down the track, freezing as he sees me a little way down the path. He's mainly in a hallowed silhouette as the sun beats down from behind him. He turns his head towards me and flicks his ears from side to side, listening out for any unwanted visitors but his predators are long extinct, leaving only us to interfere with his species. He edges down the path for a few metres then stops once more; I don't think he sees me as a threat, not at this distance.

The young Roe Deer buck stands and stares at me and I return the stare. His coat looks rusty red in the late light as it sweeps across his back. He ambles slowly, placing one foot delicately and purposely in front of the other one, until he merges with the wood and seeps within the dark, bronze coloured bracken and disappears. This part of the wood is thick with trees and overgrown with Brambles and, for a moment, the light is darkened as it struggles to break through.

There's a warm glow of light coming from the gap at the end of the track and I continue up towards it, looking back down the path where the remaining butterflies are resettling back on the edges of the track. At the end of the slender track is an old kissing gate, between the woods and the open field that leads down to a collection of meadows that look like they are untouched; many wildflowers mix with the tall grasses. With the wood at my back, the view opens-up in front of me as Rooks seem to fly up from everywhere as they stream across the horizon to their roosting sites like waves of black smoke, bellowing across an industrial sky. The croaky calls from the Rooks linger long after they've disappeared behind the distant woods.

I walk past the first meadow which has grasses almost as tall as me, until I reach an old farm gate which is partially covered in Ivy, and a Blackthorn hedge stands firm either side to border the second meadow. I scan the far edges of the meadow as a Fox sits upright in the corner under a dead looking Oak tree, as the late summer shadows cast across the quivering meadow. The Fox seems in no hurry and is staring in the direction of the setting sun which is just visible through the finger-like branches. A Barn Owl, which I hadn't noticed when I first arrived, sits almost tucked into the trunk, about halfway up, and the scene is perfectly set with the meadow in between us as I wait patiently for the show to begin.

The sky's been clear almost all day but now the clouds are moving in as the sun departs. The Fox also leaves as he squeezes through a gap in the hedge leaving behind a Fox shaped hole. On that cue the Barn Owl shakes her wings and leans forward before falling off the tree and gliding effortlessly towards a randomly placed, lone post, in the middle of the meadow. She stretches her feet forward to meet the post and her talons grasp it to stop instantly. She looks around the meadow like she's surveying everything with dark, almost black eyes; her vision's not really the greatest but her astute hearing more than makes up for it. I crouch down and try to remain as still as possible as the slightest crunch on the ground will draw her attention to my presence behind the gate. Her head tilts from side to side as she stares longingly down to the burnt yellow grasses, and then she's motionless as a Hare comes in and out of view through the shorter grass at the edges, before disappearing through the same hole in the hedge the Fox went through.

Meanwhile, the ghostly Owl stays statuesque in the middle of the meadow as I await her next move. The light is changing around her as the newly emerging clouds add a dark gold to the sky as they sweep in from the place the sun's left behind. She turns to face the area where she flew from and gives me a full view of her back with its buff coloured patterns, matching the late summer grass, and she's off. With wings outstretched and stiff she glides with very few shallow wingbeats, low across the field towards the corner, then banks suddenly, frantically quivering her wings as she hovers just above the tallest grasses in the meadow. She stops flapping and hangs motionless for a second before tilting her body and dropping like a stone into the grass and out of sight. A minute or so passes by and I'm not sure if she got her prey. Then she's up again, a few hard flaps and she's clear of the grasses and purposefully flying in a line back to the post in the middle of the meadow. A light breeze is coming in from the west as the grasses sway, drifting over and catching their tops, also just about ruffling the feathers on the head of the Barn Owl.

With the sun now long gone, the light is failing rapidly to keep a hold as the first star, all be it dim, reveals itself high above the Oak wood. The Owl swivels her head sharply around and stares intently at the base of a clump of vibrant rushes. She leaves the perch and drops at an angle with talons stretched out, towards what must be a peeping vole or mouse making a noise beneath the grass. She hits the ground with force, and in full view, mantles her broad, bronzed wings over the patch. She sits still briefly, before rising again, clutching something pale brown in colour; she heads once again to the post. This time she has her prey firmly grasped within her talons. She has her back to me again and unlike the Otters from earlier, she is not playing with her food, and in no time at all, she swallows the small rodent whole.

She sits still with the light breeze at her back that occasionally ruffles her head and back feathers which are now becoming increasingly darkened by the lack of light. A Blackbird sits on the top of a Blackthorn Hedge to my right and lets out its final vocal before wedging himself past the prickly thorns and into the thick of the hedge as a relative of the Barn Owl hoots out like a slightly blocked trumpet to announce itself to the night. The Tawny Owl's call doesn't go unnoticed and before long it's responded to by another Owl a bit further away, calling from the wood with the Poplars from where I came, looking back at the Owl on the post, whose pale, front coat is starting to dim as the sky turns to face the night. Then, she turns her head and gazes, for the first time in my direction and then away. She rises on her stiff wings above the meadow and wavers up and down as she shakes her feathers a bit like a skimming stone. She's flying with intent towards the Oak and the dividing hedge. As she flies a little higher, above the line of the ground, her silhouette breaks into the deep night-time blue as she drops into the field beyond this one and draws my day to a close.

Hometown Otter

When I was young, I used to climb the local legendary Oak tree that stood tall beside the open field at the bottom of my road. Being the one that reached the top was essential, getting that title of king of the tree. I would play in the cornfields and make up stories of an alien invasion that never materialised. I'd cycle with my brothers as far as our legs would take us, feeling like we were a million miles from home, when really we were just down the road; little legs pedalling as fast as they would go until running out of breath and whizzing down the big hill that led to the canal with the old mill. We would often stop off at the old church and explore the many paths that led through the farms and nearby allotments. From there we would usually end up at the large pond which was like a Jurassic swamp to us; it sat just in the grounds of a garden centre and that is where we would search for Newts that lived there in their hundreds. These Newts are like little aquatic dinosaurs and catching one at that age was the stuff of mythology, especially when it was the male with his jagged crest down its back, tapering at the tail with an explosive yellow and black blotched stomach.

I remember, one day on the way back from the pond with a tub full of Newts which were all destined to fill my dad's fishpond, we took the shortcut through the overgrown church gardens, and there it was, my first wild Fox which was lain dead in the opening to a track that led to the farm. I turned its head over with a broken stick to see its face; the white muzzle fur meeting the burnt orange and finishing with a nose as black as night. Untouched and with no visible wounds, it just lay there wet with a stiffened body from the night before. I remember stroking the fur and it felt coarse through my fingers, but still soft. The paw felt grainy on the pads, but the claws were sharp as a thistle. My first ever wild Fox was dead and exposed in the old farm track.

Other days we would walk through the Bramble-strewn alleyway, behind the old houses that led to the open area of overgrown grass and patches of wildflowers where we stopped near my house to search for Slow Worms under pieces of tin. We tried to catch Butterflies and Moths for our makeshift butterfly farm in an abandoned shed where three or four Peacock and a Small Tortoiseshell butterfly that had over-wintered in there for shelter from the cold, hanging dark and motionless in the corners of the wooden frame, coming out of hibernation when the warmth reached the patched-up shed.

One of my earliest encounters with nature was when I was sitting on the short grass in the back garden, gazing up at every passing cloud with the warm sun on my back and a ticklish breeze on my neck. I stared upwards at the clouds as they morphed into fire-breathing dragons and breaching Whales in the sea of blue, in the days when clouds had a softness to them. Turning my head away from the sky, I noticed a small, dark-armoured casing like an alien in a cocoon hanging from a twig in my dad's colourful flower border. As I watched, every now and then, it twitched in the sunlight and I couldn't look away. I had no idea what was going on with the miniature alien invader. I waited and wondered as I was sure I would be the first to encounter this new species. It seemed to darken its outer shell, and then within minutes, something resembling a claw broke free of the armour, a body pierces the shell next and breaks free, its wings closed, damp and crumpled against its hairy body, motionless for a few minutes as it starts to dry out in the warmth of the spring sunshine. Starting to gently unfold itself like origami, its wings are laced with flecked powder and the darkened shape is exploding into glorious colours, bright orange, mottled with black, white and yellow with a delicate blue edging; it was a Small Tortoiseshell butterfly. It felt like minutes, but I must've been on the grass with knees pressed deeply for at least an hour.

That's one of the earliest and most beautiful memories I have, and I don't know how much of it was real. After this I would always be fascinated by caterpillars and collect them in old ice cream tubs and feed them nettles which used to fight back with its own nippy sting. Most of the caterpillars turned out to be moths, like the furry little one which turned into the most wonderfully patterned Garden Tiger moth, with wings spread out like the coloured markings of a giraffe, a deep red warning to ward off predators. As an adult, I've found a few of the hairy caterpillars and hatched them out too - I just don't see as many as I used to. Maybe there are fewer around, or maybe I searched for them more when I was younger.

We would occasionally venture up the hill with the lone, Sweet Chestnut at the summit, past the big houses on the green, then down the slopes of the farm track that would lead through the wood and end at the big river. It was wild and open, free to explore its sliding banks and the great weir which split the river in two. A bridge led to a small island where cows would graze and from here you could see how huge the river was. Sand Martins would nest in the sandy banks and Cormorants, like small

Pterodactyls, would dry their wings up in the old dead tree overhanging the weir. We would carry our bikes over kissing gates and fences and cycle until we saw something worth stopping for, which happened a lot. Days seemed to never end and everyday was an adventure.

I remember me and my brothers, army-rolling through short grass and weaving around Gorse bushes to get to the legend of the corrugated iron sheets, reptiles would be found under them looking for warmth and shelter and if we were very lucky, we would find something more impressive than any prize underneath, carefully picking up each one. Occasionally there'd be a shout of a Slow Worm or Lizard, but the snake was the holy grail I sought after. One day, at the end of June, the day before my birthday, the grail was realised. We left this piece of tin till last, as most often, it produced reptiles and the occasional Newt. With my brother at one end, and me at the other, we slowly and tentatively edged the tin upwards, underneath would be hundreds and thousands of snakes, or maybe just less than twenty tiny olive green and yellow-banded beauties. They were baby Grass Snakes, and this was the biggest find in history, bigger even than my dad's legend of the albino Great Crested Newt when he was a boy. These were mini versions of the adults I'd been lucky to see before and picking up a handful of maybe five or six, they wiggled through my fingertips which kind of tickled. I'll never forget their smell as it was pungent and really overpowering but I loved it. The scent would stay on my hand for days, no matter how many times I washed it off, but I liked the smell remaining and would take a sniff sometimes before I went to bed. Every time I find one now and smell that smell it instantly transports me back to that day. Don't think my mom was too keen on the smell or the snakes being brought home in ice cream tubs.

Meanwhile, many of the little serpents had slithered away under the overgrown Brambles so we put the ones we had back under the tin and let them be. I'd check on the tin over the next few days but there was never more than two at a time. The Grass Snake was one of my favourite creatures when I was a child and still is now.

Years later, I went back to that childhood playground; I explored the area of the river with a different way of looking at it. It's still a beautiful and free place to be. The large pond at the Garden Centre had halved its size and signs had been put up warning of the dangers of deep water. The corrugated piece of iron had disappeared in the twelve years since my last visit. Everything else seemed roughly the same, the magnificent Oak remained tall, the church and the farm were still there as was the huge expanse of my childhood river in the peak of autumnal colour. I'd managed to borrow my brother's video camera and headed out down the river, at the bottom of the woods. I took a slightly different route from the one I took as a child. Clambering over large fallen trees and following a loose path through a barrage of Nettles and overgrown Himalayan Balsam to reach the water's edge, finding gaps through the trees to see the glimmering water. A pair of Great Crested Grebes used to display in the widest part of the river during early spring. Perched on an old broken jetty I could see the trees on the other side of the river, they looked like they'd been painted with autumn's paintbrush, dripping with deep oranges and rich browns. Leaves were falling into the river and joining the mass of autumn gifts that have collected from up-river. The clouds look heavy, finally bursting, drops of rain starting to fall, the season looking even more vibrant and fresh.

Amongst the reds, browns and yellows, a tiny splash of blue, hiding behind a burnt orange breast, its jet-black dagger-like beak is angled downward towards the water with intent, almost blending in with its surroundings surprisingly well, raindrops from the rain make small, dreamy circular patterns on the surface. Quicker than a heartbeat, he leaves the branch and arrows straight, dagger first in the shallow edges of the water. Colours of blue, brown, orange and green explode as it hits the surface, like a blurry splash of orange and blue watercolour dripping on a page.

It's under for a second, then crashing back above the water and flapping fast upwards and back to the small overhanging branch from where it came. A flash of commotion, then it's like nothing happened. Another diving attempt and he's become restless so flies down river in the direction of a fishing jetty to try his luck there. Seeing a Kingfisher dive on a beautiful rainy autumn day is something that has, and will, always stick with me. It was the first time I ever saw a Kingfisher dive and I can still hear the sound as the little blue bird hit the water.

Heading back, it felt like I had restarted my childhood again as an adult in a place that felt like home;
I would sit for hours in this wood just to be part of nature. I feel accepted and welcomed here.

A few years later in the early morning, at the end of spring by the river there was a dreamy layer of mist; it was like winter was still present, if only for the first hour of the day. The sun rose but would stay hidden behind the deep banks for at least thirty minutes after breaking the trees on the bank. Spiderwebs were hanging like decorations from fences and gates and looked covered in jewel encrusted dew and sparkled when the sun finally climbed high enough to break through the mist to reach them.

The field was covered in a hardened frost that stretched halfway up the hill to the grounds of the old Manor House.

I sat on the edge of the river and watched as the mist caressed the surface and guarded the lone Ash tree on the far bank. It wouldn't be long until I'd hear the sharp little call from the Kingfisher as he always called up and down his territory first thing in the morning as a ritual. In my head I'd see an Otter coming out of the mist and onto a sandy spit in front of me, but it never happened. I've seen many Otters away from home, but none here, but that's what I craved. There were many signs that they were here, catching them occasionally on a trail camera, but I wanted to see one here with my own eyes; an Otter on my river in my town.

I set myself the challenge to see one before I turned thirty, which was still a few weeks away, and with the days so long I knew it was my best chance. Days in late June seem never-ending with very little time for the dark. Some mornings I would get the feeling that I had only just missed an Otter but was always rewarded by the sound of the Kingfisher. I was by the river most mornings over the next few weeks and I was treated to some brilliant frosty Fox viewings and a Barn Owl that hunted the meadows near the river, but no Otter.

The next time I was going down was on my birthday. The night before, I'd decided to stay up through the night and head down just before three o'clock in the morning. The night had been cold and littered with stars so I knew the morning would give me a little more light to play with. I felt like a wide-eyed dreamer as I headed towards the river. On my way down I bumped into two Hedgehogs snuffling around and courting in a road-side verge. I wonder If they thought, what on earth are you doing down here at this time as they were startled by my presence; no other person was seen on my journey. I'd made it down to the river and twilight blue was lighting the dark, a Tawny Owl called, late for him, but early for me, from a small plantation. It was the last sound of the night before the diurnal animals took over, with a sleepy sounding Robin yawning his way through his first vocal and a raspy call from a watery Moorhen.

I headed to one of my camera traps that I'd set up the afternoon before; it was in a tree over-hanging the river, aimed at a fishing jetty where an Otter has recently been leaving its mark. A quick check and then I would sit somewhere and hope to be rewarded. I climbed up the tree and through the tangled web of branches and onto the largest, lowest branch. I reached over to get my camera and I was fully aware that if the precarious branch broke, I would be the mammal swimming, not an Otter, it's taking an age to untangle the string that's holding my camera in place. From here I can see straight up the barrel of the river and ripples made by early fish catch my eye. After fiddling to get the camera down from the branch, something at the end of the barrel catches my eye, it's a larger ripple but as there are many ducks around, I told myself that's what it must be. My eyes were still straining to focus on the dark tinted blue, but as the trailing ripple began to form a perfect v shape, I started to believe that this could be the moment I'd been waiting for. As I was still hanging over the river and had no time to move, I clung on tightly to the branch just above the river's surface and hoped I would go unseen amongst the branches, my fingers rubbed green from the Lichen as I gripped tightly. It soon became clear that this was an Otter and although still far away, it was heading in my direction and edging ever closer. The sight as it came closer of this wonderful creature in beautiful light was beyond my heart's belief. The river mirrored the cool blue of the sky as it got closer still, until it was within a few feet and heading right for me, I couldn't believe it as it swam at arm's reach underneath me. I could see its streamlined back and paddling legs, and in the stilled silence of dawn, I could hear her breathing through her nose. She stopped under me and sniffed the air around her looking up and down river, but never upwards. She pondered on various smells then swivelled around and headed towards the shallow water of the jetty, sprainted on a rock just before the jetty; it's a good place to communicate with other passing Otters as it connects the river to the canal. She came out of the water and up a muddy bank and up onto the jetty. She had a little shake and sprayed water everywhere and then headed off, up the slope and away. The moment was over. It felt like I could suddenly breathe again. I waited, still hugging the tree for a few minutes then made my way down, out of the tree and dusted myself off before perching on the jetty myself to reflect on what had just happened.

The sun's still not risen above the distant farm fields, birdsong is filling the air and echoing down river, it's half four in the morning and dew has covered the meadows attached to the river and given it a covering of something quite magical. Banded Damselflies are almost frozen by the droplets before the sun warms them up and they can become active and fly. I watch as one cleans itself from the still water that covers it, he sparkles like a thousand diamonds as the sun lights him up. I pick up a drenched looking Bumblebee and hold her up to the morning sun, her wings begin to dry as she trembles to warm herself up and she quivers her wings like they're attached to a little motor. It's only taken a few minutes but she's dry and ready to leave the tip of my finger and off she goes.

Everything feels so beautiful and I greet every bird and insect I see with a warm good morning and inform them all its my birthday but with no response, apart from a Robin who sings back at me. It wasn't *Happy Birthday to You* though, just its usual sweet song. Five o'clock and the first Buzzard hits the air and is swiftly joined up high by a Kestrel who alarms frantically at the passing raptor who's just stretching his wings in the early morning sun. The male Kestrel has a nest nearby and does his best to usher the Buzzard away. A handful of Jackdaws, with their silvery armour, fly from behind the bend in the river toward the lone Ash tree. The laughing call of the Green Woodpecker rings out from the nearby playing field and the Wren matches it with a big-sounding vocal which shouldn't come from such a tiny bird; it has a massive anthem of song that dominates the river's edge. The Damselflies are now airborne and dancing like fairies, just above the long grasses and Bulrushes and I'm leaving the riverside with the memory of an unforgettable morning. An Otter in my hometown and on the river where I played when I was young.

The River

It's late afternoon and I'm armed with a large bag as I've decided to stay the night beside the river so that I can catch the early dawn. I find a place that's got a little protection from the wind and is clear enough to pitch my old tent, the ground is still soft and it's easy enough to stick the pegs firmly in the ground. I throw my bag down and empty the contents onto the floor, unroll my bright blue sleeping bag and a hoodie for a pillow. The weather's changed since this morning and within a few minutes the rain beats down against the roof of the tent, it's a soothing and scary sound at the same time. A Tawny Owl lets out its iconic call and is joined by another one from across the river, it sounds like there are a few surrounding the tent, but it's still only two. The Owls call less frequently over the next few minutes and seem to have moved further away and into the conifer wood down river where I've seen them roosting before. The rain is joined by a wind that blows hard enough for the tent to shake a little.

I get as many short periods of sleep as I can through the seemingly endless wind, I can hear it blowing through the trees and swaying them from side to side, it whistles up the river and pushes the side of my tent against my face. I had a decent hour's sleep in the end, but now I'm up and surprisingly wide awake. It's still before dawn and I'm letting the sounds fill my ears before throwing on my clothes and venturing out of my makeshift, sleepless home for the night. The rain is still coming down but not as aggressively as it was through the night and the wind has finally given up. This day seems to nestle between the winter and the spring, even on these wetter days it can bring its own unique charm. The Blackbird, Wren and Robin still belt out their morning tunes through the patter of raindrops, nature doesn't stop and put up an umbrella or stay inside. The rain isn't falling with a cold bite of the fading winter but more of a spring warmth, a soft mist begins to form through the arch of the old medieval bridge and gathers pace as it covers most of the water's surface before reaching the height of the trees that flank the river. After a few minutes, the bridge is barely visible through the smoky morning mist. I sit on a damp mossy brick wall at the edge of the weir and stare longingly into the water, I can see more clearly at the weir as the swirl at the bottom of the cascade isn't allowing the mist to loiter and settle so it moves further down river. A Little Egret is on the far bank, her white gown looks bogged down and has lost its frills, she's joined by a very vocal Dipper looking mainly black but he's flanked by a rich chestnut colour and perfect cloud-white chest, constantly bobbing up and down but doesn't stay long, he's not got time to sit on his rock and pose as he's got a nest to construct. The female calls for him, and off he flies, low to the water and up under the bridge where a nest is being built in a gap in the brick of the arch. The rain suddenly shoots down from the clouds like bullets, hitting the water hard and with feeling. For a few minutes the bird song is silenced by the rain, they have nothing left to say until a Kingfisher breaks a hole in the wall of rainy noise with its sharp three peep call as it flies down river, leaving a trail of flashing blue and an echo behind him. Suddenly the bird song is back and coming from every tree as the rain turns back to a light drizzle and the last of the mist evaporates. The distant, lone Willow stands in the clear at the bend of the river looking like a natural marker. I make my way up the brick steps to the old bridge, the smell of Fox wafts up from the nearby wood and where I almost slept last night. A Little Egret has been disturbed by something in the scrub just up from the bank and launches into the air and flies to the other side before perching on the branch of a fallen tree and is followed into the air by three Mallards that alarm call loudly as they go. The creature that caused the bird to hurry away is making the Nettles move as it works its way through, the culprit will soon become clear as it's nearing the edge, the last Nettle folds away and out pops a bouncing baby Rabbit. All that commotion for such a tiny animal who's just happily feeding away on the lush river's edge.

The brief calm in the weather is over and the next band of rain is falling steadily onto the river, a pair of Great Spotted Woodpeckers are chasing each other through the canopy of Birch trees and making their presence known with loud, chipping calls. These two have paired up and it won't be long before eggs are laid in the hole in the main tree they're squabbling from. I gaze down the barrel of the river just watching these stories unfold until I spot the wonderful and unmistakable shape of an Otter. If the Wren, Kingfisher, little Rabbit and Woodpecker, amongst others, were a brilliant warm up, then this is the main event, straddling the bend and gliding under the vibrant lone Willow was that unmistakable shape. The Otter was still a way off but heading towards me and the weir, I had time to slide down the bank and get myself well hidden behind a trusty tree stump and wait. The Otter sinks, then emerges in the middle of the river, twists three times in the same spot without any real attempt at fishing, she just looks playful under the overhanging branches. I crouch further down and as I look back, she's been joined by another two streamlined shapes cutting through the early water; this must've been the mother and the cubs of the river I've been watching of late. As they approached the bridge, the mother slipped under the water and the two cubs quickly follow in unison. I watch as the cubs play, rolling and entangling together, working their way slowly through the arched bridge to the place in the river where the water almost stops, well-covered in Reeds, Water Lily and Flag Iris and was a good place to forage through the underwater roots for small fish, Eels and sometimes a Frog. Occasionally, one would go astray when it foraged further away from the other two and, by chance, when it emerged, the other two would be under the water. For a few moments he would think he'd been abandoned and cry out for them until the little cub was relocated by its mother and joined by its siblings, often quite amusing to watch as they were never too far away. That high-pitched little whistle carries across the water and can be heard from some distance and it is always lovely to see them reunited, they would embrace as though they'd been away for weeks, gently touching each other's faces and tangling together once more before setting off down river again. Just before they reach the weir, an adult male Otter is coming up the river towards them, possibly the father of the cubs, it's always interesting to see what reception a lone male gets from a protective mother as sometimes it can be aggressive. On this occasion, she seemed pleased to see him as she swam in his direction and greeted him with a succession of excited peeps and one sharp vocal came back at her. The cubs were left on the other side of the river to continue foraging and had no interest in watching the adults' game as they rolled and played above and under the water for a few minutes. Splashing about in the thick, grassy water roots getting it stuck between them, emerging back up to the surface like two aquatic monsters from the deep, draped with the reeds around their heads and covering most of their bodies, finally dislodging it as they swim around in circles and parting before carrying on in opposite directions. The mother joins the cubs and hugs the bank to reach the top of the weir, the male casually made his way in the direction from where he came towards the bridge.

I decided to change my direction too and headed back up-river with the male Otter as I didn't know much about him and his habits, he seemed uninterested in fishing and just went in mainly straight lines near the wooded edge of the river, the trees gave me shelter from the rain and made sure I had many places to stay hidden as we made our way past the bridge. At the bend, the Willow was dripping almost waterfall-like into the river as the male stopped on its exposed roots briefly to scratch and mark his territory before slipping back into the flow of the river and carrying on. The further he got from the bridge, the wilder it became, the path had come to an abrupt end and I had to scramble through Brambles and over a fallen tree to stay in sight of the river. Eventually, after what must've been a mile, following him up the stretch of river, he stopped near a smaller weir for a good root around in the nearby vegetation, coming out of the water at the top of the weir to smell the air which still had a lot of rain in it. He carries on past the weir, and after a few minutes, he leaves the water behind and headed up onto the steep-sided wood, filled with drenched Oak, Birch and a Weeping Willow. I've lost him as he made his way through the wood and up the bank, he must've gone off to rest and that's where I left him. I stand still, surrounded by soaking trees and a blanket of Wild Garlic and Wood Anemone around my feet, the leaves are being pushed back by the few lingering drops of rain. I head back through the wood, the Brambles and over the fallen tree to re-join the path, the rain has begun to slow right down and looking back towards the end of the river I could see a distant patch of blue sky reflected on the water. It seemed to take much longer getting back to the old bridge than I remembered but I'm back at the spot where I last saw the mother and her cubs. The water around the weir is choppy and it's hard to see if an Otter is there or not, I remembered sitting by the weir for thirty minutes before realising there was an Otter in it. I sit again on the same rocky wall and after ten minutes of seemingly staring into empty swirling water an Otter pops up, then another, and then a third. They hadn't got very far at all, seemingly spending a lot of time fishing and playing, as the sun finally made an appearance through the rapidly breaking blanket of cloud. The trio headed off further down river, playing along the way.

The early morning mist had made a return to the surface of the water and almost blanketed the river like a white cloak which could be taken off just as quickly, this atmospheric touch has changed the scape again and lit up the river to an almost gold colour created by sunbeams coming through the trees, silhouetting the three Otters as they floated downstream. The cubs come near the water's edge and a fight breaks out between them, loud and furious peeping coming from both, rolling and tangling in a different way to the playful games of earlier. The mother comes in between them and breaks it up and they go to different sides of the river carrying on their journey, occasionally looking over to each other with jealous little eyes if the mother was slightly closer to one of them. The mother lands herself onto the banks of a shallow, stony beach and is joined by one her cubs who nibbles her tail and rolls over onto his back over, and over again. The other cub is still trying to catch small fish just up-river in the vegetation and eventually heads over to the beach to join its mother and sibling. All three head from the beach to a well-exposed network of old Oak roots. It looks like a child's imaginary fortress, something I would've dreamt up when I was young. The mother leads the way and clambers up the main branch that's reaching down into the water like a slide and the first cub isn't too far behind, the second cub looks smaller and less confident as she tries to scamper up with her shortish legs. The rain has turned the branch into more of a water slide and she loses her footing and slips backward and hits the water without any grace at all, just like an upside-down cannon ball. She looks startled as she returns to the surface and swims around the mass of roots and waits in the water with her head raised in the air waiting for the other two to finish playing.

The Spring sun has climbed up and over the top of the last of the clouds and burnt away any remaining mist, the river flows with a different beat as it opens-up to its widest point, trees are replaced by open flower meadows where a smattering of shining yellow Lesser Celandine and Cowslip line the banks. It's a wonderful picture as the mother, flanked by her cubs, meander round the open bend of the river and leave a silvery trail of ripples behind and this is where I'd leave them. I sit on an ivy-hugging stump and breathe in the sights and sounds all around me, it's like a thought-provoking piece of music with an adventurous side show. I close my eyes for a second, feel the light breeze and sun on my face and just listen to the song of the river, a beautiful end to the start of the day.

The Tracking of Wild Tarka

I can't believe I'm even here, it doesn't seem that long ago I was pouring over the pages of the book that was set here; I've come a long way from being trapped inside my head in my room, but here I am, overlooking the woods and the river that Tarka called home.

Taking the wooded trail to the old stone aqueduct, I happen across what looks like a mouse climbing up the side of an old Ivy-covered Oak. Its stuttery movements and small, curved beak reveal it be a Treecreeper, edging its way up to almost the top before trying its luck on the adjacent tree. Calling high at the top is a small flock of Bullfinches, and just visible is the vibrant and bold pink chest of the male, glimmering against the sun. As I fall out of the well-covered wood and onto the open, gravelly track, a Pied Wagtail flits in front of me, waves his tail before launching into the air and calling as he goes. I reach the aqueduct and the river looks a long way down; it's a great vantage point to see the curves and swaying of the river. Cattle churn up the grass on the banks of the river. I can see Kingfishers fizzing up and down in an almighty hurry, usually the result of many hungry chicks to feed. Dippers are hopping from rock to rock, then skimming under the water in the search of Caddisfly to feed on under small stones. The sun is nearing its highest place; it will sit and batter the sun tops of the wood. Three Buzzards soar on thermals and rotate together like a slightly out of control spirograph in the sky. Looking up, it looks like a wonderful place to play and lose a little control. My eyes are fixated on the birds, and I wonder, as I so often do, what it would be like to fly and feel that much freedom.

Heading away from the river and over farmland on a small path that cuts through the fields giving me an open view over what feels like almost half of the world. An acrobatic Swallow is twisting and turning, inches from the top of the short grasses and corn and is joined by the slightly smaller Sand Martin, Rabbits run for the safety of their burrows as I approach, a bit like lead shavings with a magnet. The far side of the field is separated by a slightly raised bank which is scattered with old, grey rocks and a few large holes. My eyes squint at what looks like the rufous, red shape, of a Fox. To the right of the shape are three smaller shapes of slightly lighter red and they are on the move. As I skirt the bank, and edge closer, I can clearly make out the Vixen and her three little cubs soaking up the sun; they have a prominent position for surveying the area at the far side of the raised field. The Vixen raises her head in my direction as if to say you're okay there but any closer is too close. I take the cue and leave them to enjoy their peace and the view from the fields, all the way to the sea which is where I'm heading.

Leaving the open field and sloping off through a rocky, banked Gorse path that's descending fast, I walk past a handful of sun-worshipping Common Lizards that are residing, motionless on an exposed, pale tree trunk. I reach the end of the path and enter the Valley of Rocks which looks like a sea cliff sculpture park, with two giant ominous natural rock pillars guarding its entrance. Walking in the short grass, I come across a black and white diamond marked Adder lapping up the sun's rays and tasting the air with its forked tongue to see if I'm a threat. I assure him I'm not, but he takes no chances and slithers away and under sun-dried Gorse. A Green Tiger Beetle scuttles across the bare, sandy soil with its shimmering, bright green body armour and ferocious looking jaws, making it a formidable tiny predator. I clamber up a few steep rocks and pull myself onto a flat rock that overlooks the coast. The rock looks precariously balanced on the edge, but it's more in the mind, and its plateau is a perfect spot to sit for a short while and watch the world go by. I'm alone up here but not lonely when I have the whole world in front of me, or at least a small piece of it. The sea looks calm and has patches of turquoise and fragments of dark navy, in between the soft summer blue. The raucous sound of the Raven stirs my attention as it flies underneath the crag, the sun changing its black into an oily, purple sheen, its diamond shaped tail quivering as it glides in the tidal breeze. Flying close to the crag, swerving in and out, it's joined by its life-partner from above and they engage in a synchronised, aerial display, flipping upside down and calling loudly at each other, coming together to a mid-air pirouette like two dancers; an aerial ballroom display if ever there was one. High above, and just below the low, wispy clouds, is a sharp, pointed-winged anchor of a silhouette; it's spotted the Ravens down below and lets out a fearsome cry to warn the two sky dancers of its presence. In seconds, the anchor has transformed into a teardrop shape and is falling fast towards the crag; it's set its sights and aims right for him at full velocity. He pulls up just before as one of the Ravens flips on its back and turns its clawed feet skywards towards the oncoming Falcon. The Falcon lifts high, then aims itself again at the giant Corvid, they are both whirling around like a flying game of cat and mouse; no intent to harm, just an aggressive game. The Peregrine has finished harassing for now, and on stiff wings lands on a prominent outcrop on the crag and surveys his territory, like a king on a throne. I'm paralysed as it stares-me-down and cuts right through me. He turns away, surveys his area once more; the slate grey, bluish back and black and white chest barring, draping black moustache and cap that cloaks the white like a hood. With both of us prominently poised on the edge, he turns away and looks higher up the crag, with intent. Just visible is the back of his mate who's sitting with three chicks, he's their protector and is keeping the territory clear from any danger, ever alert in case an intruder should get too close, when he'll spring into action and give them a warning until they leave which they so often do. The aerial dancers are back, and he launches to the sky once more; they are nesting just around the corner and these games will go on all day, and all summer; they go together and often share territories. When they both have young on the wing, they will practice the life skills they'll need on each other, but for now, calm has been restored on the cliff.

Gulls are quartering the sea cliff on the breeze and disturb Jackdaws as they tumble, one by one, off the rocks, all calling together as they fly around the outcrop and out of sight. The Peregrine is back and looking more relaxed with its world. I leave him to watch over his craggy world and scamper down off the flat rock on the edge. A slightly more careful approach on the way down is needed and I'm watching every foot and hand hold for weakness. The sharp end of the yellow Gorse catching my arm with a warning and I'm back on the track and heading through the guardian pillars of the Valley.

I'm following the water as it flows downstream, leaving the smell of the coast behind. Either side of the river looks ancient and steep, sloping with old Oaks to meet the river below. Time has woven a meandering waterway and, nearing the bottom, it joins to a second river and straightens out. A Grey Wagtail, bathed in dappled light, bounces from rock to rock. An old, stone bridge, greets me and reflects imperfectly on water. Mayfly and small fish make tiny ripples on the surface and late Dragonflies patrol the banks to keep their territory under control. I'm heading through a timeless piece of countryside and checking all the prominent spots for signs left behind by the Otter. The smell of Wild Garlic is whirling off the slopes of the wood but can't overpower the occasional whiff of a Fox that has passed through, not long before. Reaching another wonderfully crafted stone bridge, I take a moment to stare, straight down the middle of the river. Everything feels so alive, bird song is coming from everywhere; from the Dipper on the rock, to the Song Thrush hitting high notes at the top of an old Yew.

I amble further down river where the river stretches and thins, with many exposed rocks. I take to the water's edge and walk barefoot through the shallows, turning the occasional rock, hoping to reveal an Eel or Crayfish. The water is gentle and crisp as it ripples through my toes, and my soles are caressed by the pushing, grainy stone. I sit in the middle of the river on a large rock, the river echoing the sound and the history of the book in every tree, bridge and ebb and flow. I wonder what it's like to call this place your home; to rely so much on this river and the wood for food and shelter.

I wade through the small rocks and get back on the track. A few hundred metres up-river is a bigger stone bridge where the occasional car goes by, the sound is muffled, near the base of the bridge and it is still birdsong that dominates the noise, with a few brief squeaks from Mice and Voles sifting through the undergrowth. I find an old, mossy stump just down from the birthplace of Tarka and take my seat and wait. Opposite me is an old Oak with its roots reaching down into the water. Either side are grassy banks with clear Otter slides, worn from the top, to reach the water. A tiny Wren is busy weaving in and out of the roots, I can just make out the sounds of many calling chicks coming from a clump of Ivy just above her, she's frantically searching for food to keep up with their high demands. It won't be long till she roosts and can, at last rest for the short darkness of the midsummer night. Sitting still and looking on, you can hear and see all the things missed when in a hurry. A couple of Ladybirds climb to the top of a Thistle, its small, red armour is bold and pressed against the lateness of the sun.

There's slight movement in the water from upstream, coming from just behind some fallen Willow roots and I freeze, the ripples are bouncing off the bank, but I can't quite see through the tangle of Willow. The water is still again, and I wait patiently for the creature to reveal itself. A minute or two goes by without a flicker and then a louder splash comes from the direction of the river's edge, wedged against the side is a female Mallard and her mate, foraging in the shallows of the river. The Drake's head is eye-catching and a glorious green that turns to iridescent blue as the light bounces off the water, five little Ducklings come from almost nowhere and join the pair, whizz around each other pecking at everything that moves. Stretching out their little heads to try and reach the tiny, flying insects, with one or two taking to the air for a brief second, then plopping into the water again. The five of them hurriedly follow their parents out into the middle then slowly paddle up-river, under the bridge and onto an exposed Oak. The sun is heading behind the distant rolling hills, and the drop in the sun is creating a shallow mist that hovers just above the surface as the daylight enters the beginning of its end. I wait in the stillness as the sky is gathering a subtle army of clouds high above.

Without warning an Otter has emerged all fluffy and dry from the base of the Oak, she looks wary and alert as she surveys up and down the river and just sits motionless for a few minutes, her blotched pink nose twitching and her long whiskers ruffling as she shakes her head. Two small brown, round shapes appear from behind one of the main roots; two Otter cubs blinking in the last of the light, edging out tentatively and nuzzling up to their mother who's looking much more relaxed than she was, but still sitting with her head raised. The cubs are almost half her size and although this doesn't look like their first venture to life outside the holt, I doubt there's been many before. Placing their tiny paws on the back of their mother, she responds with gentleness, eyes flitting up and down river and focusing hard on a loudly offensive Magpie that passes by. One cub spots the Wren in the roots and looks fixated on the small brown bird, it feels serene for a few minutes until all three look startled as a Kingfisher pierces the still and flies close to the bank near the Otters, its call echoing up the river as it flies, the brilliant flash of blue darts upriver giving a blurry mirrored reflection on the water, passing the Oak and Willow and through the arches of the old bridge taking his sharp call with him.

The mother of the cubs makes the first move and slips into the water without a sound, they sit and watch as she rolls in the water in front them, urging them to join her, letting out a short whistle to entice them over but they look comfortable between the roots. Eventually the smaller cub wades into the shallows and, not to be left out, she's joined by her sibling. All three splash about in the muddy, shallow side of the river and peep loudly with an almost excited noise. The female disturbs an Eel and has it in her paws like a bar of soap, squirming in and out as she tries to hold it still. The cubs jump on her and she loses her grip and the Eel slips away to survive another day. One of the cubs, heads across the river and is almost eye-level with me as she sits on a raised rock; I can see her whiskers twitching and the final glimmers of light in her young eyes. She looks right at me and tries to figure out the shape lying at the base of the mossy rock. Her eyes are locked on me for a moment, she turns away as her mother calls her back to the shallows, and they set off upstream, hugging the bank as they swim. The mother leads the line into the middle, and the two cubs almost merge as they head against the flow of the water; three beautiful streamlined silhouettes leaving v shaped ripples behind, passing the vibrant, overhanging Willow and as far as the bridge until I lose them round the bend of the river.

As the darkness begins to win the fight against the light, it is time to leave the waterside and the Otters behind.

An Otter Under Starry Skies

The late summer sky is still hanging onto a midnight blue colour before reaching the next step of pitch black. The moon is a long way from being full which allows the stars to shine at their brightest without the moon stealing their light. Heading almost blind and guided only by what's lit up above me, I find the track that's sandwiched by thick Gorse bushes. The overpowering sweet, almost coconut smell that they give is being carried around on the light, night-time breeze. I lose my footing in a wet patch of moss and would've fallen but for a perfectly placed Rowan tree and its helpful, slender trunk to grab hold of, but my left foot is drenched and squelches and squeaks with my next few steps.

I reach the path's end and come across a fallen tree; it must've been brought down in the recent high winds but there are no such winds tonight. I clamber over the bare branches and reach the dark, rocky coastline to meet the sea and look out to the lonely harbour sat in the distant inlet. Looking south I can see Jupiter and Venus are sharing a kiss; they rise and move closer together, almost shaking hands with the crescent moon as they pass by. It's peaceful, with only the occasional call from a half sleeping Oystercatcher to break the quiet. Looking up reminds me just how small I am, getting lost in the galaxy of stars above me, no unwanted noise, just the night lit up by natural light. The occasional flash from a meteorite scrapes through the seemingly still stars heading north. It's the peak night for a meteor shower and that won't be the last one I see tonight.

The sea is resting and feels endless with only the slightest silhouette of the far away mountains breaking between the sea and the sky. There's another flurry, a quick succession of stars shooting from west to north and one of the brighter ones reflects briefly off the sea. The sky has now let go of the midnight blue and it's entered its darkest moment, like a slack water. This moment is sitting in between the tides like dusk and dawn. I move further around the coast trying not to slip on the rocks with the little glow from my torch to help light the way. The eye shine from Rabbits beam back at me as they're caught in my light as they scurry back up into their seaside burrows.

I know this path well by day, but at night it's transformed; the beautiful Oak that splits the stream feels more timeless and looks like it's reaching out for something. Across the small rocky stream is an old stone wall and two Oystercatchers sleep with one eye open on the darkened rocks of the shore, their heads are tucked firmly into the wing with just a small amount of blood red beak showing. As I approach carefully, they both open their eyes simultaneously and stretch their legs and stand up in an alarmed posture until I'm past them and then they both resume their position on the rock. As I turn back, I can see them resting their beaks under their wings again and I leave them in peace.

I click my torch on again to see how close I am to the water's edge. The rock that protects the land on this part of the shoreline looks scarred with pale criss-cross marks etched in by natural vandalism from the relentless tide and storms over many years. Further on, I settle down in between two giant boulders that have Foxgloves sitting just before the water's edge and are tinged with a flicker of light from the harbour. I stare upwards to the North Star as more and more stars fall out of the sky, some with long bluish tail streamers. Looking up at the stars makes me feel more alive, especially on a night as clear and calm as this one.

The distant ferry lights reflect perfectly on the water's surface and there is a faint glow of light on the distant horizon coming from the nearest town on the mainland. It feels like most of the world is fast asleep with only me and the creatures of the night awake beneath the biggest sky I've ever seen. The slightest touch of pale green dances in the northern sky just above the horizon. The Aurora has come out very briefly to play and is gone just as quickly as it came, leaving the sky to resume its black state. It's not only falling meteors in the sky as a couple of Bats glide and swirl in the air then skim just above the surface of the water before heading furiously over my head towards the darkened wooded hillside. I sit still and fiddle with the smoothness of a pebble in my hand. A screeching call from a Tawny Owl behind me makes me know I'm not alone. Another Owl calls back and I listen to their conversation over the next few minutes as they scream back and forth to each other. Then they stop, it's absolute silence; enough to hear the tide turn like a creaking cog being put in reverse.

Then, through the reflected light is an unforgettable but distant sound, a sound that's instantly recognisable as an Otter, magnified by the quiet. As my heart rate quickens, I see the still water in front of the harbour turn to ripples as the near perfect reflection of the overnight ferry is shattered and shards of orange and green tickle the water. Then the still has returned as if nothing was out there. Sitting here in absolute silence I think I can hear my racing heartbeat as it thumps out of my chest. A minute passes by but the water remains a flat calm and yet another star rattles through the sky. I wait, still, trying not to make a sound. An eternity seems to pass by, and a blanket of cloud has been thrown across the northern part of the sky; it's like a door has closed out the night sky and locked away the stars. The cloud spreads thickly and quickly across the sky.

I've never heard the sea so quiet, just the gentle lapping of waves against the rocks in front of the harbour as I uncoil myself from the ground and head closer to the old stone pier. Suddenly the door's now ajar above me as a star or two, peek out from behind the newly formed cloud until the gate blows open and the stars light up the night again. Within minutes it's as clear as it gets and it's not long before the next meteorite shoots down. The cloud's gone as quickly as it arrived from the northern sky.

I scramble over the oily rocks and tall grasses and huddle down next to the old pier walls beside an exposed jet-black rock and wait and listen. I wait for an age and convince myself the Otter's moved further out and around the coast and away. I set up my camera and point it straight up, the slight click from the camera bounces noise off the sea. Then, four meteors, in a handful of seconds, light up the northern sky as they fall behind the hills. Further out from the harbour, more ripples; they are Otter shaped ripples. He's half-way out between me and the harbour but heading in a line in my direction and the ripples are leaving a v shaped trail in its wake. He dives under and the surface returns to a still state, if only for a moment, until he breaks the surface and shatters the calm sea again. This time he has a small fish and is keeping himself afloat to munch his way through his night-time meal. It's a wondrous sight as he's lit up by a combination of the stars and harbour lights. He dives into the dark water once again.

I take a moment to look around at three hundred and sixty degrees of beautiful night sky until the Otter reappears much closer to me than the harbour. Then a peep in my direction, I wonder if the sound of the camera has got the Otter intrigued? The Otter heads in my direction at full speed and clambers up onto a rock a little further out from the old pier. The distinctive shape of the Otter breaks the distant ferry lights; his head is pointed towards me and his tail is angled, curved and upwards. He sits there glaring at the noise coming from the pier walls as if waiting for that noise to move. After a minute or so he decides the noise isn't going to move anytime soon so he slips into the water and drifts in the direction of the clicking noise on the shore. He's only about twenty-five feet out and he's motionless as the water around him flattens to a perfect still. He lets out a snorting sound from his almost submerged nostrils and dives rapidly under the water. He's not up again after his usual twenty-five seconds, and now it's been almost two minutes. He must've drifted away and I'm left feeling exhilarated as the first glimmers of faint light are skirting the horizon to the east. Then, without a sound or warning, the Otter emerges on the edge of the rock I'm sat on. It's still dark but he's very visible and breathing with an intensity. I can make out his long, draping whiskers and his inquisitively dark beady eyes have been lit by the falling moon behind me. He's staring at the shape on the rock; he must know I'm here, but curiosity has taken over. It feels like an eternity but it's only about four or five seconds that he's sat almost face to face with me. I hold my breath and stay as still as I can, he snorts loudly in my face and glares at me momentarily before hunching his shoulders back and turning back into the flat sea and out of sight.

I've lost him under a plethora of stars as he's hidden by the sea. I scan towards the harbour and around the shoreline but I feel he's gone.

The light is beginning to gather faster with a pale blue fused with yellowy green colour sitting where the sun will eventually rise. A final shooting star falls behind the now more visible distant jagged mountains of the north. The turnaround from darkness to light is swift at this time of year and it's not long before a small party of Puffins fly low up the Sound followed almost immediately by a Gannet on a mission. I catch a fleeting view of the Otter exiting the water between the harbour and the pier and up the small stream and away behind the tall grasses. A couple of welcome clouds join the sky as a Wren shouts out its morning song from the end of the pier.

The turnaround is complete as the sun dressed in a deep orangey red, breaks the skyline and ignites the sea and surrounding scape. The night is over for now as a new day has begun.

The Frozen Canal

It's nine fifteen in the evening at the beginning of January, the sky's been dark for some time. As there's less day than night at this time of year, it gives more of an opportunity to watch more nocturnal animals at play in more sociable hours. I'm heading a mile away to an area that, when I was a child, was a meadow with a canal and a stream, but now it's an estate with a trickle for a stream. Houses sit where the meadow was, but the old canal still runs through the middle. As I pass a cluster of detached houses on the main road, I can see Christmas is being removed with discarded tinsel and wrapping paper spilling from the bins, trees are abandoned to shed pine needles on the pavement, and the twinkly lights that were woven in hedges and trees have been removed for another year. The clear sky has added a bitter sting of cold to the air and, for once, I have gloves on and a scarf wrapped tightly around my neck. Stars are just visible past the streetlamps as the moon climbs above the Sports Centre roof which gives a yellowish dusting, the cars come to a halt as the traffic lights turn from amber to red as I walk by. Before long it's back to amber, then green, and, like wind-up toys on a racetrack, they're gone. The noise is reduced enough to a hear a Song Thrush belting through his repertoire from a television aerial across the road. The sweet song is broken up by the screeching from a bus as it brakes at the bus stop, just ahead of me, across the driveway of the last house. Before the canal is the unmistakable shape of a Fox, sitting upright, watching the traffic and looking for the best chance to get over to the other side so I stop at the edge of a well-kept Privet hedge to see his next move. The streets are empty but there's still a steady flow of vehicles, so he waits; his ears are pricked up and he's intently focused on the road watching as cars stream by waiting for his moment. The lights behind me have turned to red and he seizes his chance, the moment they went to amber he knew what was coming and darted across without hesitation; not running in fear, but more a speedy saunter the way only foxes move. On the other side he marks his territory up the side of a bright red post box and strides over to the entrance of an Ivy-covered house with an overgrown front garden and sniffs at the gate. He's watching up and down the path almost like he's waiting for something. I notice a lady with a pushchair heading in his direction, and as I look back at the Fox he's vanished. In the time it took me to look up the road and back he must've skulked into the shadows of the garden and away, clearly spotting the approaching lady way before I had. I remove myself from behind the hedge and carry on towards the bridge over the canal. Just before the bridge is a footpath that leads underneath. Suddenly the light has gone, and the canal is almost black with only a slight reflection from the moon giving any light. Just after the bridge, the canal is at its widest point, and the far side shallows look like a small ice rink with footprints from Ducks and Moorhens weaving around in a circular pattern with breadcrumbs resting on top.

Thick Brambles and Hawthorn line the towpath until the first set of Locks near the factory entrance. A lonely streetlamp lights up the Locks and a Robin sits proudly upon a kissing gate and sings loudly through the freezing air. Just before the second bridge, the water is still and there are patches around the Bulrushes at the edges where it's frozen; it might freeze over completely before the sun rises again. The roots of an old Oak cover a small embankment that twists partly into the water on the other side. like the edges of the Bulrushes, the roots of the Oak are also frozen in the water that gives a dark winter's fairy-tale feel to them. I imagine that, deep into the night, the Otter swims around these roots and up the embankment.

An elderly couple walking their dog, both wrapped up in their winter coats, as is the little dog, with his stripy jacket and they're quickly followed by a flashing light from a late-night cyclist who whizzes past me. I reach the third canal bridge which is just about lit by dim underpass lights, graffiti heavily marks the sides of the bridge and adds colour to the dull grey. One of the small pieces of street art is a bird of prey, broken into pieces of a heart which raises a smile. Otter tracks are obvious on both sides of the bridge and at the entrance to a water flow a few minutes down. Beside the bridge is a concrete block where I'll be sitting for a while in the hope an Otter will pass through under the cloak of almost darkness.

I can just hear chimes, bronze and copper clanging from the nearby church as the clock turns ten. A few cars pass over the bridge and their tread echoes underneath like a rumble. There's movement on the other side, beneath the overhanging Bramble. A few ripples of water come from next to the wall and a sound like a gentle kiss peeps out; it's the sound of a Moorhen and she appears briefly before scrambling up onto the bank and slinking away into the pitch-black undergrowth. Sitting here, almost engulfed by concrete, I still feel the anticipation, as I would by the edge of a rocky shoreline or a wild river. The Otter inhabits so many diverse places, but its needs are always the same. I almost jump out of my skin as a scream comes from the direction of the bank in front of me; although I can't see her, it's coming from a Vixen. This is the mating season for the Fox and the females calls out with a blood-curdling cry; Foxes only have a short window when the Vixen can mate and are very vocal at this time of year. She again produces the call and it's met by a barking response from a nearby dog Fox who keeps close to her in case any rogue males encroach on his territory, an area he would've defended for most of the winter and isn't about to give it up now. The male comes out of the shadows at the top of the bank and his silhouette is briefly caught by an orange streetlight as he disappears over the top and out of sight. The Vixen screams from opposite me every so often, and despite straining my eyes, I just can't pick her out but the occasional faint bark from the male suggests he's still not that far away. Then it stops. I'm not sure if she's moved away or if she's still in the thicket of the bank but it's fallen silent. Half an hour goes by and the temperature plummets even further, but I'm still sat on the concrete in a crazy hope, rather than expectation, that I'll catch a glimpse of the Otter that leaves the tracks behind. The church bells sound out once more and I count in my head till I reach eleven, don't think I'll still be around to hear them ring out for twelve.

I haven't seen anyone walk over the bridge for a while and a car going over has become rare, despite being in the heart of the City it's now only natural sounds that I can hear. A Tawny Owl calls from the tall trees that line the old factories and a Swan chatters to itself from down the canal. Nature reclaims the day in this part of the City. My eyes are still trained on the still water and edges of the bridge, the only movement is coming from small fish rippling the surface. The absolute peace is broken by a group of lads heading home from the Football Ground pub and it's got me thinking of heading that way too. It feels well below freezing and the cold has finally bitten through my gloves. I'll give it five more minutes then I'll leave it for another day, just in time to beat the ring of the bells again.

Ripples are coming up the canal in the direction of the bridge, I can't see what's making them, but I just about make out the movement of the water as it approaches. I crouch down a little bit trying to make myself more compact and less visible, then the sound I wasn't hoping for, the quacking noise from a drake Mallard and he becomes obvious as the light catches him as he passes the line of the roadside lights. False alarm, and he looks like he's sleep-paddling as he swims by with only one eye open; that's the signal to follow the Duck and head on home. I trail the Mallard for a short while before he turns into some long grasses to presumably take rest and close the other eye. Now it's just me and every noise from the hedges is magnified and a little scary; it's funny how darkness makes us so much more fearful of what we can't see. Just before the second bridge I hear the clock from the church strike twelve and this will be the last time I will hear that tonight.

The Locks are empty, the Robin has vacated the kissing gate but is still singing from the top of the Hawthorn under the streetlight. It's quite common for some birds, especially Robins, to sing through the night, mainly in urban areas using artificial light. The scraping sound from my feet on the gravel path is all I can hear now; it's a sound that in the day you wouldn't notice, but in the dead of the night with the Robin behind me, it's all I can hear. Up ahead I can see the main lights from the road and the arch of the first bridge. In the icy shallows the waterfowl footprints have been joined by what looks like fresh Otter prints that weren't there earlier when I passed; four pads and a slight line where the tail has dragged. An Otter has passed through in the last couple of hours, maybe heading up the canal and away from town, both directions of the canal end with a river with many tributaries along the way. There's a faint shadow on the wall of the bridge and it's an Otter-shaped shadow; she's fully out of the water and striding through the bridge. I freeze and watch as she spraints on the path and sits motionless for a minute. I wedge myself as far into a Hawthorn bush as I can without getting impaled by the pointy thorns as she looks up and down the canal before slipping into the icy water under the bridge. I lose her in the darkness as I wait, trying to make as little noise as possible. She emerges in the shallows opposite me, and, in the silence, I can hear her deep breathing. She sits on a clump of bent down grasses which is barely lit by the streetlight by the road above the bridge, she's feeding on something and as she turns to get a better grip of the squirmy, snake like animal, it's obvious it's a good-sized Eel. Eel is a favourite meal of the Otters that inhabit rivers, canals and marshes particularly at this time of year as it is hard for Otters to find food here so an Eel will be a welcome meal. I can the hear every crunch as she makes short work of her slippery feast as she slides off the ice and cuts through the inky dark water, head above the surface, she paddles slowly down the canal, so I detangle myself from the Hawthorn and head in the same direction, sticking tightly to the hedge so as not to be seen. I can't see her trail on the water so presume she's dived once more. Minutes pass by and I'm not sure whether I can carry on or stay still in the hope she'll emerge nearby. I can see the second bridge and Locks lit up down the towpath so walk slowly toward them hoping she headed there, and with more light around, it would give me more of a chance to catch another glimpse. A short, sharp peep echoes down the canal coming from this side of the Locks; it's one of the most beautiful sounds I've heard and as the only noise I can hear, this amplifies it. It's not the noise of the female, but a cub, I've heard it many times before and it's never forgotten. I pick up the pace and follow the sound through the dark until it stops as quickly as it began. I'm straight in line with the old Oak roots and I'm sure that's where the call came from, crouching down, once again trying to merge into the thickets of the twisted Hawthorn hedge, I wait and wait and wait until a single bell rings out for one o'clock, at the same time the peeping begins once more, it's more raspy and frantic than before, and it's coming from the roots. I can just about make out a figure of what looks like a young Otter, he's bouncing around and in between the weaving roots and, as he pops up to the top, I get my clearest view. The cub is tiny, the youngest Otter I've seen, not sure he's old enough, or ready to leave the natal site. The slight moonlight catches the head of the youngster and gives him a sheen to his fur. His peeping continues in a flurry until it's met with a response by the female coming up the canal. The call from his mother has sent the peeping and movement of the cub into overdrive and I can see the little bundle waiting to get to his mother but fearful of the freezing water. The female gracefully leaves the canal and onto the roots where the cub is ready to meet her at the edge. The cub's calls now sound joyful as he tries to clamber all over her, merging into the female and it's hard to see anything but one Otter. The female looks upwards, stretching out her neck and yawns as wide as she can, her mass of whiskers and nose are caught beautifully by the winter's sky and have a silvery shine to them. She huddles her young under her again and the movement stops as they almost become part of the exposed roots, making them almost impossible to pick out. The peeping has stopped, I stay crouched for a few minutes in case they reappear but there's no movement. My heart rate begins to get back to some form of normality but that was simply breath-taking to witness. That's only my third and fourth Otter near the City in years and I'm heading home now to defrost.

From the River and Out of the Shadows

One summer night when the light lingers longer than normal and the night feels like a short encore to the day, the warmth from the all-day sun leaves a haziness on the horizon. I'm sat on the slope of a small hill; it's not a great height but it's everything I need. The river below swerves and bends under the bridge and through scattered woodland, finishing with open fields at the drop of the sun. A Sparrowhawk glides through on the light thermals and gets the attention from a few Swallows and Sand Martins who show their displeasure at the presence of the aerial predator. They chase and harass the hawk as a unit, until he's beyond the hill and out of sight, and they gather up high in the late summer sun; looking around from here, I could be at the top of the highest mountain. The light from the sun is fading but is angled at the ground and the river to show it in all their glory. Through a sprinkling of trees, at the river's bend, I can just make out my tent peering through the branches; my accommodation for the night. Looking down at the fields to the west, they have that wonderful yellowish, green colour they sometimes get from the long summer, the grass is long and interspersed with blood red Poppy and Oxeye Daisy and is teeming with swooping Swallows making the most of the last of the daylight. As the flying insects emerge before dusk, out of the corner of my eye, I notice a pale shape on a post on the fence line; my excitement builds as I'm hoping it's a Barn Owl but it's very distant. I hastily scamper down the slope of the hill, tripping over Rabbit holes on my way, through a crisscross of Birch trees that border the field. I peer out from behind the last line of trees and my eyes scan intensely to the corner of the field where the possible Owl was. There's nothing on the fence post and the grassy field looks empty, apart from the lingering

Swallows. Something on the far side is moving the grass around and edging through, I'm eye-level with the tall grass but can just see it's being disturbed from its stillness. There's plenty of light left in this day and the sun isn't ready to leave just yet, but the moon can't wait around forever and rises just beyond the field, amongst the Oak trees in the distance. It's an almost full moon, and it's slicing behind the trees with a handful of light clouds and makes for an atmospheric backdrop. Through the grass, in the foreground, I can just make out the black ear tips of a Fox; it's weaving its way through the grass, but only the ears are visible; that's what was making the grass sway. She's moving through slowly but she might become more visible as the middle of the field is slightly raised. Still no sign of the possible Owl but I'm waiting excitedly for, hopefully, a full view of the Fox. Two Collared Doves flee from the middle of the field in a hurry, and a Rabbit shoots out the verge in front of me and disappears into the wood behind me. There she is, stepping up onto an exposed mound in full and beautiful view, standing upright and proud with her long, flowing bushy tail. She scans the field and the edges but hasn't noticed me with eyes firmly fixed on her. Being fully focused on the Vixen I've missed the Barn Owl which is silently quartering the river end of the field, showing exactly why they're referred, so often, to be – ghosts, with the ever-rising moon in the background, it's quite eerie and beautiful. Her wing beats are so shallow she seems to just stop in mid-air and then float; I've never seen an Angel, but I imagine she would fly just like this. She turns and I can see the cornfield buff on her back, and pure white underneath. The sun's just disappearing behind a distant church but flickering one last time on the Owl, just before saying goodnight and heading out of sight. The Owl hovers momentarily, as if to catch the last glimmers from the sun, before falling sharply to the ground in the grass beneath. The Fox is still on the mound and has lay down with her head raised; she isn't far from where the Owl went down but is paying little attention.

She sits for a few minutes in full view, like she's taking a breather and surveying all around her, including the Barn Owl who is back in the air and gracefully floating over the summer grass with the background sky turning to a deep pastel yellow now the sun's gone from sight. The Owl is heading straight in the direction of the Fox in what looks like slow motion; she's head on with me, with straightened wings and darkened eyes. The Vixen sits upright and stares upward as the Owl carries on her course and, for a few seconds, they are lined up together as the Owl flies low over her head. The Vixen just stares at the pale figure just above her head that arches around the end of the field and lands on the post I first spotted her on. The Vixen is now becoming more active and is silhouetted against the inky blue sky as the light fades. She's off with a restless hunger in her eyes as she struts down the slope and vanishes into its dense wall of taller grass. The Owl is back in the air and quartering once more on the far side of the field with a casual flight pattern, until suddenly, tilting her head and dropping her shoulder, then plunging into the meadow with speed, she's down and out of sight for a minute before pushing her wings up and rising upward with something small in the grasp of her talons. She hurriedly leaves the meadow and cuts through the sparse Birch trees and out of my sight; she'll have chicks to feed nearby and it's going to be a long night for her. I think it's time I left to locate my tent before the light completely leaves me.

The transition time between light and dark feels so different from any other part of the day; the colour change, the drop in temperature and the departing of the diurnal and entrance of the nocturnal creatures. The first creature of the night to appear is just up from the river, on the open grass, which is turning damp from the clear skies; it's the Hedgehog, one our most beloved mammals, he's shuffling and sniffing about on his way across the field, stopping just before the edge, by the Blackthorn bush sniffing the twilight air in the direction of a teasing moon. Sitting, almost motionless for a minute, as I relay the story of the Fox and the Owl to him without much response, apart from the occasional twitch of his tiny black nose, I try and get the Hedgehog to stay for a while but he's got a busy night ahead and ambles almost comically away into the undergrowth. I cut through the gaps in the hedgerow that leads to the river. The water level at this time of year is low and, without much rain, it runs with a soothing sound. The final Blackbird is serenading his good night song and then a silent, calm falls on the riverbank.

I find my bed for the night, sitting nicely in a clearing by a handful of young trees by the river's edge. I haven't got much with me, not even a sleeping bag, just a jumper to keep me warm as I'm not planning on sleeping much; I wasn't going to waste the light and it's not going to stay dark for long. Sitting in my tent I can hear everything, it's such a wonderful way to hear whilst being unobtrusive and lets the wildlife behave as normal. As the darkness and silence fall around me, I'm stuck in a moment of pure peace until something breaks the calm and is making a cracking sound on the wooded floor. In the direction of sparse trees at the water's edge, I slowly unzip the front of my tent and poke my head out; I can still hear the noise, and it's getting louder. I venture quietly onto the softened grass in front of the tent and creep toward the noise, trying not to make a sound. The cracking has stopped and all I can hear is a couple of Tawny Owls sounding out in the distant wood. Through the finger-like branches, I can see a dim shimmering coming from the floor, so I head off to investigate. The shimmering is caused by the full light of the moon shining on a large, half-eaten Fish; it looks like an

Otter has brought the Fish out of the river to eat. As there was no sign of the animal and there was still plenty to feed on, I decided to stick a trail camera to a tree to see if the Otter would come back to finish her catch. I left the camera attached to a small Birch, aimed at the Fish and retreated to the sanctuary of my tent to wait until first light, sitting and just listening to every crackle on the wooded floor. Every now and then the Tawny Owls would start calling. A little while later when the faintest of inky dark blue gives just enough light; I return to the camera to find that the Fish has gone but no animal was in sight. I removed the camera from the tree and couldn't help but feel excited to see what the camera had captured. As I scrolled through expecting to see the returning Otter, I saw a few Voles, a little Wood Mouse and then the main culprit turned out to be a very fortunate Fox. He wasn't there long, just skulking in and dashing off with his find. It was so great to see this opportunist at work; he must've smelt the Fish from a distance and got lucky on his search for food for his Vixen and cubs nearby. The Otter's done the hard work and had a lot of the large Trout but now the opportunist Fox and his family will finish off the rest.

This feels like the coldest part, but it's when the air feels at a resting point, time is trapped beautifully between the night and the day, the inky blue sky is merging with a soft lilac as twilight approaches and there's an oily, reflective pattern on the river, and the fields are filling with light. I walk the riverbank being accompanied by the glorious bird song from the early morning Robin. Fresh Otter tracks are pressed into the exposed mud on the shallow bank of the river, just under an old Willow and a slide next to them where she's climbed out of the water. She's used this route many times before and it leads to the nearby canal. The Robin is joined by an array of other birds trying to make themselves heard above the rest; they are all drowned out by the loud calls of the drake Mallard who seems very angry at something. Behind a small set of Reed stems on the canal, a cheeky, early morning Moorhen weaves out to greet the boisterous Duck and the quacking stops. Nature is waking up fast and Goldfinches are calling in a small flock and take full advantage of the abundance of the Thistle heads, red, black and white meet a beautiful golden trim as they flutter down from the loose Birch trees. Sunrise is still over half an hour away and already everything is bursting into life and trying to be the star of the show. Next to audition for the limelight is the drumming sound of the Great Spotted Woodpecker, smacking his head against the old bark in a blur of red, white and black high up in the deadest of ancient Oaks. He calls out after that head-banging and flies deeper into the wood. A pair of Swans do an impressive flyby, not far above the treetops, and the sound from their heavy wings echoes up the river. I catch a quick glimpse of the Barn

Owl from the night before, heading back over the field and back to the roost site in the old wood where a mass of bird song is starting to filter through before the sun breaks the skyline. The river, apart from a lonely Moorhen near the bank, seems quiet and almost devoid of life. For a moment the chipping call of an alarming Wren in the water scrub is the only sound. Even the flow of the water looks to have almost stopped, breathing gently on the straight and moving freely round the bends, kissing tree roots as it goes. In the corner of the arch in the river, is a swaying of the water, just enough to catch the eye as it slightly upsets the reflective calm. The slight rippling of the water carries on around the bend and onto the straightest part of the river, a trail of bubbles start floating frantically to the surface, meandering and circling and leaving behind a bigger swirl on the water. I follow the bubbles from side to side like a game of hide and seek until they disappear under a fallen tree and stop. Circular ripples come from the roots like mini waves and the briefest glimpse of the brown, silky tail of the Otter as it disappears into the watery undergrowth, then nothing.

The river's as still as a flowing river can be, so I sit and wait. The side of the river is littered with overhanging trees, reaching down to grab the water, whilst on my side it's open with stinging Nettles, Thistles and sparse, tall grasses, giving me an uncluttered view upstream. A simmering, golden light touches the tops of the grasses and hits the pink Thistle flower heads as the sun's first light breaches the ground. The Otter has vanished without leaving a trace and I'm left watching the early morning insects take flight above the water. It would be easy to think they were midsummer fairies, dancing and sparkling as the light reaches the surface and bouncing off their tiny wings. Whilst watching the magical little performance, another ripple further up-river catches my eye and an Otter rolls on the top of the water and then under once more. I wade through the Thistles and thrusting Nettles towards the place she went under and then a swirl appears fifty metres further up, where the river is split by a wise looking Willow which had an exposed, large branch and a hollow underneath. Finally, the Otter comes into full view, stretching out the water and up into the base of the Willow; she almost shines as the light reflects off the water onto her wet coat and the sun tickles the Otter's nose with a gentle light. It's a wonderful sight to see her at the end of her day.

I'm on the opposite side, hidden by an old stump of an Oak but it's protected by a handful of Nettles and they're not happy about me pushing against them, so they fight back and sting my hand with little barbs. The irritation isn't breaking my focus on the Otter though who's rolling around and drying her fur on the hardened roots, she looks up the water towards the adjoining river which is much larger and wider than the edge of the tributary that she's on. Looking across the water she stares just past me, I slowly turn my head around, and approaching me, completely unnoticed, is a small herd of young male Cows who seem to have me cornered but are just being inquisitive. I look back and the Otter has gone, slipped away into the early morning river. The roots are left with water sprayed on them from the early visitor, a short but glorious moment with the Otter is over.

I can hear the birds more clearly now as the high-pitched, sweet song of the Goldcrest comes from a Weeping Willow and a Chaffinch chatters loudly. Maybe when the Otter was around, my focus tuned them out as now the birdsong is almost deafening. It suddenly feels late in the day, but it's only just turned five am and I'm heading home after a wonderful display of beautiful wildlife; this time belongs to them.

All the other contestants and performers from the Barn Owl to the cheeky Fox, the rising moon and the setting sun, then the early bird song, the head-banging Woodpecker and the light on the river and inquisitive Cows have all led to the Otter who has come in late in the day and stolen the show.

The Track

It's late summer on the island and the track that takes me up through the woods has that autumnal feel; it doesn't matter which season I walk, it still has that feel. The trees near the top are plastered in moss all the way up to the main branches, they have a timeless quality and they soften the view. Behind them is the view down to one of many bays which opens-up and out to sea as far as the distant mainland. Further on and around the bend is a short rocky slope that needs to be scrambled down to re-join the track, its loose soil and crumbly rocks make it a bit tricky but I'm soon back on the well-trodden track. Further on and the trees give way to a small cottage wedged between two rocky slopes and in front of it lies the most beautiful, peaceful and charming little bay, bordered by dark rock jutting out on one side to a small worn jetty on the other. It feels secretive and well-hidden and is barely visible until you're there. It's one of only a few beaches made up mainly of sand on this side of the island. I sit just up from the water's edge and flick a few small, brightly coloured pebbles and watch the trails they leave behind in the sand. A couple of young Gannets are circling up high in the large expansive bay, normally brought closer to shore by storms out in deeper water but here it's calm, isolated and sheltered. One of the Gannets dips its wing and arrows toward the water at full velocity, plunging head-first with its spear of a beak and cutting through the surface leaving a heavy splash behind. After almost half a minute, he returns like a cork to the surface and sits there for a short whilee seemed unsuccessful in his attempt and it will take him a season to perfect it. Wings beat hard against the sea and feet push frantically backwards until he's airborne and his search for food goes on. The mountain beyond the Sound has mist tied around it, just below the summit like a scarf, and apart from that there's barely a cloud to trouble the sky. I leave the enclosed little beach and walk onto the old jetty; its many missing pieces provide a refuge for Otters to rest as I've seen them use them before in between fishing trips. The high tide has the end of the jetty engulfed in water, so I head away and up onto the flat rocks which divides an area of shrubs and tall grasses until it clears to reveal Otter rock just off the point. I named it that owing to its many signs that it's well visited by many Otters. It sticks out prominently at the corner of the last bay before the plantation and is the perfect spot to sit and watch in two directions. The rock here is hard and looks and feels like it's been here for a million years for many creatures to stare out from. I could imagine a Bear taking a rest on top of its grassy bank or a Wolf pack gathering to survey their area; not likely these days or on this island but the local wildlife now is just as spectacular. The high water is beginning to be teased out as the tide turns loosening its hug on the sea rocks and lowering ever quicker. Seems like as good a time as any to leave Otter rock as the water leaves the land exposed once again.

I re-join the loose track that heads through some Sphagnum Moss that squelches as you sink into it and, at this point, it gains a bit more height above the sea. Just ahead is the Pine plantation guarded by an old iron gate without any obvious purpose. Through the iron gate that makes a loud and offensive noise as you enter; it doesn't matter if you pull it fast or slow it still lets out that sound. As I enter the wood, the Pines close in and shut out almost all the light. It's twisted and overgrown and you're lucky if you make it through without getting snagged on a thorn or two from an over-reaching Bramble. Despite its seemingly inhospitable nature it's still quite charming and when I reach the last of the Pines and pull back the curtain of needles, the walk through is well worth it as it opens-up and light floods back. A large grassy bank covered in pink and purple Heather with a smattering of young Birch and Alder awaits on the other side.

From here you can look right down the barrel of an expansive bay
and out across the Sound to the ominous looking peninsula,
another place to just sit, watch and wonder as a small assortment
of clouds come into view for the first time today. The grass is
soft, and I could lie here for hours whatever the weather. I'm lined
up with the tide and I can see how fast it's pulling away from the
shoreline and leaving seaweed and rocks exposed. Soon it will give
back the isle of the Otter that was lost under the high tide. More
wispy clouds float in from the north and south until they collide
in the middle, high above the Sound. Their shadows ghost along
the ridges of the mountains beyond the peninsula, leaving the
Heather-drenched grassy bank behind. I make my way down a
steepish slope that skirts between the Pines and the shore where a
boulder layered with bright green Moss lies in the middle and is
one of the Otter's favourite sprainting spots. I step onto the
pebbles of the bay which are slippery, as until recently, they were
submerged in the tide and haven't dried. Being relatively careful
where I'm stepping and trying to look out to sea at the same time
is tricky but after a few near slips and slides I'm onto the grass. As
I tread, the grass underneath me bounces as it spends half its time
under water, it's like a sponge. A few mountain Hare reside here
making use of the short salty grass; isolated on this island they've
adapted to come down from the mountain slopes to live at sea
level. There's none to be seen today. Jumping off the grassy

bouncy castle and onto the prehistoric looking rock, which is almost jet black and looks like volcanic lava having tiny divots which make climbing over it easy. I'm now approaching the largest bay off the track which includes the isle of the Otter. I named it that as it was a reliable spot and would almost always have an Otter or two lounging about on it or foraging in the rich waters that surround it. Female Otters would sometimes leave cubs on it, like a safe crèche when they went fishing further out. I'd sit from a distance and watch the young Otters sleeping and playing together for quite a good length of time, until the tide turned, and the island would need to be abandoned. I find the rock that I always sit on, which is in the centre part of the bay, and look in all directions. Each way has something to please the eyes. The silence, which has spent most of the day with me, is disturbed by the passing ferry; the voices from the travellers onboard are carried across the sea like a happy murmuring sound. The engine sound finally ceases as it disappears around the headland and it's almost silent again but for the gentle sound of the tide on rock, a cheerful Robin singing from a fruitful Rowan tree and a solitary Bumblebee buzzing by. I sit for a short while on the rock that's plastered in different coloured Lichens until I hear the distant and mournful sounding song from a Seal. It's eerie and sounds lonely, with a hint of desperation, then it stops as he submerges under the water.

I leave the rock and meander towards the rocky bay, the cracking sound of shells beneath my feet instantly calms me and brings the memories of this place flooding back in waves; I'm on my own here but I don't feel lonely, I never have. The sun's been pouring down, and the wind's being kind, but it still has the feel of a shift in the seasons. Leaves have just started to gently trickle from the trees in the wood behind me as the slightest breeze comes in from the north. Small birds begin to gather up for the winter after the breeding season, particularly the sweetly vocal Long Tailed Tit, flying from tree to tree like a small piece of pink candy floss attached to a lollipop stick. Then the call from up high that I've been waiting for, the chattering call from Pink Footed Geese arriving back from Greenland to overwinter in our slightly warmer climate. They chatter to each other as they fly, always communicating during their journey of a thousand or so miles. It's always exciting to hear and see the first arrivals, like a marker of the first day of Autumn, they are flying very high and I lose them between the clouds. They'll be heading further south than here, looking for open farmland near water. At the water's edge, many Pipits are flying low from rock to rock and foraging on the tide line. Then a bird, not much bigger than a Pipit, is heading my way and darting close to the shore, instantly unrecognisable as a regular, it flies low and skims the head of a preening

Oystercatcher. It's suddenly very recognisable, if not very unexpected, its dagger bill and shape give it away as a Kingfisher. It flies within a few feet of me and as it passes underneath, I can see his brilliant electric blue stripe, searching for Otters out at sea and straining to look up for Geese. That was the last thing I thought I'd see today.

Still buzzing from that unexpected encounter, I take some more time out to watch this corner of the world from yet another rock. I hear distant rumblings as a Red Deer bellows out its pre-rut roar from the woods, high above the bay in preparation for the battles in the forthcoming months. In the last ten minutes there've been two massive signs that colder days aren't far away. A passing Dragonfly skims by as a reminder that summer is not quite finished yet; I'm almost getting confused as to which season it is. I come across a spraint that's not on a grassy bank or prominent rock but on top of a clump of yellowish seaweed, it was still fresh, about as recent as possible, without watching the process; it must've been minutes as the seaweed would only just have been uncovered by the receding tide. I stared deep into hypnotic water and scanned from the tiny peninsula to the Pine plantation, out to the island and back again but there was nothing, just a lonely sailing boat a mile out. Sometimes they would sleep just in the dip of the island, just out of view from most angles. In front of the island is the smallest slither of sand that's only exposed when the tide is low, and despite its tiny size, it's a place I could sit and stare out to the sea forever, or until the tide comes back in, whichever happens first.

The tide has now reached its lowest point and it's the furthest I've seen it go out, owing in part to the new moon which is due in a few hours. I'm seeing rocks beyond the island that I haven't seen before that have been left behind by the tide. A Curlew lands on one of the rocks and begins to call and hearing that distinctive sound always reminds me of being here, no matter where it is; takes me back to the first time I was here when a Curlew was the backdrop to a couple of Otters playing in the foreground. I can still remember the sound of the cubs calling to each other and the smell of a low tide. The Curlew flew off the rock and over towards the Sound and north away from the island. The clouds have now completely closed in but they're bright and it's casting a wonderful serene light on the water, isolated beams from the sun are just breaking through and making spotlights on the peninsula as they pass. The sun's started to dip slightly as it begins its descent and will eventually disappear behind the peninsula on the mainland, but there's still a lot of light left in this day and the tide is still to turn before the darkness comes. The lightest drizzle sweeps gently across the Sound filled with salty sea air but it's not enough to displace me from the rock. Within a few minutes the fine rain has dispersed and there's yet more breaks in the clouds, allowing even more light to filter onto the sea and touch the hillside. The light wind has a change of direction as the tide is triggered to turn back; it's got that feeling that everything is possible, it's beautiful!

My attention is drawn to a loud, raucous sound coming from just under the cloud. I make out the silhouette of a large corvid heading furiously towards the top of the wood on the hill, its croaky call and diamond-shaped tail give it away as a Raven. Further above the hill and a bit higher, are three or four other birds, two looking significantly larger than the others. The Raven heads straight for the two distinctly Eagle looking birds, by the way they are holding their wings, these must be a pair of Golden Eagles with a Buzzard, and a Crow also involved in the fracas, all of them chasing each other whilst circling in the ink-blotched clouds. The Eagles are climbing higher and higher until they've lost the others and can relax without being harassed. The other three head back towards the tall trees on the hill. The two Eagles are encircling each other with the fingers of their wings very prominent and almost touching as they go past one another, their golden manes are being caught by the last of the sun and almost shining a golden orange colour. They head up and over the high point of the wood and out of sight. The sun too has finally surrendered to the peninsula, but it's left the sky with a peachy tinge and melted onto the water and that's where my eyes are drawn. I'm edging my way around the rocky coast towards the last of the bays and to the point that looks right back over almost all the area. With the tide creeping in and the light beginning to change as quickly as each other, it's that wonderful time that I've seen a lot of Otters in. The sea has still got a calmness to it, despite the changing water, and if there's anything out there it will surely be visible.

Just before the point is a small bay filled completely by tiny shells, many of them broken up over years and a few pieces of almost pure white Coral amongst them. All the other bays have stone, seaweed or a slither of sand but this one is the only one that's different. Amongst the white is the occasional piece of green sea glass worn and rounded by the sea over time and purple and green Sea Anemone. Leaving the bay, I head for the last rock to sit on and it's on the point, it's full of soft grass, broken Crab shells and Otter spraints. The peach on the sea has turned to a rich pink and the clouds have an inky blue edging, like paint dropping into water, Gulls fly to their overnight roosting sites and the last ferry for the day sails by, heading for the mainland with lights beaming out in the fading light. The sea and the clouds are rapidly turning colder colours of deep purple and slate grey, and above the peninsula is a glow of burnt orange left behind by the setting sun. Then, without warning, the surface of the water ripples with that distinctive v shape cutting through, headed by an Otter, the sky is still light enough, and the calm of the nearly high tide is glass-like. He dives deep with that arched fluid motion that barely leaves a trace on the surface. He's under for about half a minute then breaks the water fifty or so metres away, near the bay of shells. The sky and sea have darkened to a dark inky shade and it's got that change of season feel, with a crisp cold in the air. I'm straining my eyes to see but I'll stay until there's no light left at all. On his third dive, the Otter came up with a decent-sized fish and it looks too big to eat in the water, so he paddles furiously toward the end of the point, unaware I'm tucked in between a couple of rocks. Headfirst and almost eye level, it's just his head and the fish that I can see above water as he leaves a large rippled trail in the water behind. He scrambles up and onto the rock at the end of the point, places down the fish, sniffs the air and shakes off some of the salty water from his fur, he's cautious at first, looking around and checking for danger, moving his head up and down and side to side; the breeze is helping me as it's blowing on to the sea and I remain unnoticed. He seems more relaxed and begins to feast on his catch, tearing through it with the whitest of teeth and grasping it with his webbed paws and tiny claws. He's almost becoming silhouetted, as against the tide the light is almost all gone and the first of the brightest stars comes out to play. After a few minutes, the fish has been devoured and a Gull watches on nearby in case any scraps are left but the rocky table looks empty as the Otter heads back into the darkness of the sea. He swims a few metres from the shore then slips with ease under the water. I wait for a few minutes, surrounded by absolute silence, just staring out to an expanse of darkened sea and sky. The end of the day is taking a long breath before the night begins.

The silence is broken momentarily by an early Tawny Owl calling from high up the Oak wood. The Otter by now has moved further down the coastline and I can just make out a rippled trail as he travels through the water and out of sight. A few more stars join the sky in between the broken clouds and, that's me done for the day. I've had so many wonderful moments today along the track but there's something about the Otter that makes my eyes slightly wider and my heartbeat that little bit faster.

The Snow Otter

In between the fierce winds and seemingly never-ending rain that lashes from the west, we get those crisp, still and frozen landscape days, when the sea breathes with a deep sigh of almost relief, before exhaling the tiniest of ripples. The hills look pale and closer than they normally do as they reflect beautifully on the still blanket of the sea. Today has been short as the sun has skipped just above the mountain peaks before slipping away before the entrance of the dark. The night is clear and almost dark, the waxing crescent moon is smiling down at me and I smile back with a grin on my face. The stars are surrounding the moon and litter most of the sky with their tiny illuminations, I arch myself backward to see as much of it as I can and stumble and almost fall in the process. I retreat to the warmth of my bed hoping that tomorrow will bring more beautiful light and the freshness that only winter truly gives.

It's early morning, my eyes flicker slowly as I make my way to the window to see what the day has given me; I wipe the last of the sleep out of my eyes and stare out of my window onto the seemingly dark and empty sea. Apart from the lights of the overnight ferry reflecting on the water like taillights on the windscreen through a storm, the first Oystercatcher sounds out in the bay and it won't be for the last time. There's a deep smell in the air and the clouds have huddled around the moon and cloaked the sky. The clouds are first to receive the light this morning as the faintest of Bullfinch pink falls upon them. The clouds look full and ready to burst as they turn battleship grey.

Now the surrounding hills have a faint sea mist dappling the contours as they come further into the light. The clouds burst and within minutes heavy drops of rain crash onto the rocks and sea and make a sound loud enough to disturb the feeding waders on the shore who fly up the coast and take shelter under the wooden pier. The heavy rain falls continuously for over an hour and washes the road clean but it's still blisteringly cold as the rain starts to turn to hail and is falling like tiny ice bullets. Watching the weather change so quickly is powerful, a faint sun is just visible through the white mass and is a hauntingly beautiful thing.

The pair of usual Blue Tits have arrived and look bedraggled and already worn out; they are swiftly joined by a Coal Tit who timidly gets to the feeder whilst the other Tits are taking their stash to eat on the adjacent Holly bush. Siskin and Chaffinch arrive together to join the party as the cold rain continues relentlessly to beat down taking it in turns to grab some much-needed, high energy food which is especially needed on a day like this. A flock of Jackdaws struggle to fly in line as the wind and the ice blow them around like plastic bags in a storm, managing to get lower and fly just above the swollen-looking sea, before eventually finding refuge on the lower branches of a large Spruce tree. The sky is now a mix of slate grey and peach and the ice-rain has crystallised into falling snow, flurry after flurry whilst swirling around is sticking to the road and edging the trees like icing sugar on a cake. Within minutes the snow has filled-in every corner of land and even settled on the larger rocks on the shore. I've never seen snow cover a landscape in such a small space of time. The snow is as dense as sea fog and the coast is barely visible from my window which is now half covered in ice. There's absolutely no chance of seeing the haunting sun through the blur of white and grey. The heavy flurry begins to ease off momentarily and now looks more like a coastal snow globe that's been shaken up and placed on the mantelpiece. After an hour of relentless snow, the landscape has turned into a coastal winter wonderland and the final few flakes start to fall, then the clouds are empty and have given all they have.

I can't resist any longer, so I step outside for the first time today and head straight up the track that looks and feels so different, but it'll still lead me to the shore. I tread heavily on the freshest of snow which has that beautiful, fresh crunchy sound with every footstep. A cliched Christmas card Robin sings from a snow-tipped Gorse bush and a Crow flicks and pecks at the ground under the wall, looking to uncover some food under the snowy blanket. The sea opens-up wide in front of me. I bounce along the wintry coastline, heading past the old Oak which is now plastered in a white dressing; the broken stone wall and the natural stone sculpture which lays un-moved but the snowfall has clothed it all in white.

Up, in the sloped pale woodland, stands a postcard looking Red Deer stag; he looks down on me with his coat looking even more regal behind the flurry of snow. The tide's left the shore and shallowed the sea to leave a few patches of sand which have small amounts of snow on exposed rocks but has melted away quickly from the salty, grainy sand. The makeshift wooden plank which acts as a bridge over a small stream has five delicate toes pressed into the white and tell me an Otter has not long passed through.

Washed up pieces of driftwood break up their journey and lay naked upon the tideline until the next winter storm takes them out again. I scan the sea, but the waves are dancing out of control, looking up, the clouds have reloaded and look ready for another wintry attack on the ground below. It's not long before the first snowflake hurtles past my head, followed by a few more gentle flakes taking more time, and almost floating like autumn leaves and landing on my winter hat. I can barely feel my hands and my cheeks start to feel what morning grass must feel like when it's overcome with frost and the areas that lost the snow as it melted have been replenished. I'd never seen an Otter in snow before and I wasn't heading home until I had.

The snow rarely lasts long on the coast as it melts away so quickly because of the wind and salt, so I knew I had to push on. The small exposed islands now looked like mini icebergs in the Arctic, but it was an Otter, not a Polar Bear I was wishing for. The icy tide is slack, and the dancing waves have finished their performance for now and left the sea in the calmest state. Shaking the fallen snow off and wiping ice from my face, I sit under a sheltered Pine tree for a breather; the sound of absolute snowy silence from the hills to the shore. A Raven which is just visible through the blur of white, breaks the quiet from up high and its call echoes across the Sound for miles. Another snowy blast and I can barely make out the water twenty feet in front me, let alone the hills. It's spine-tinglingly cold but bewilderingly beautiful and the falling snow is almost hypnotic as it drifts past my eyes. Icy snow looks huddled around tiny beach pebbles like it's been crocheted into a winter's pattern.

Snow makes me remember being a child and building lumpy snowmen with my brothers, so I mound a tiny one on the rock in front of me and give him a couple of pebbles for eyes and seaweed for a mouth which makes him frown. Whilst playing with my snowman construction I think I can make out the call of an Otter, very distant but just enough to stop my heart for a second. I feel the excitement build in my body and I hunker down further between the Pine and the rock. Snow begins to settle on me and now there's more snow on me than my little make-shift snowman, but it's easing off and I can just see the still of the water and some of adjacent trees. The shallow bay further in front of me looks empty and quiet with just a couple of Curlew sat on its rocky edges, looking totally unfazed by the winter snowstorm. The snow has brought the usual sounds of the coast to absolute silence, even the waves have been muted. A single screech from a passing Heron overhead grabs my attention; he's angling his wings to land in the bay further up around the coast. Still no sight or sound from the Otter, despite my constant scanning of the water and snow-covered rocky shore. A patch of floating seaweed is the only thing that's not pale in the bay, I scan it as it's a place I've seen Otters forage under before.

Light snow trickles down from the Pine branch above my head. A Goldcrest is flitting around the Pine needles and displacing the lingering snow. The tiny manic bird weaves its way through the lower branches until he's within a few feet of my head, turns to face me head on, shows off his delicate olive-green wings and, for the briefest of moments, flashes his impressive golden mohawk before it flattens upon its head again.

My eyes are alerted to movement out on the water. I just catch a glimpse of a tail disappearing into the icy tide and I wait half a minute for her to re-emerge from under the water. Up she pops and glides through the water and up onto a piece of drifting seaweed, snowflakes falling around her melt as they touch the floating mass. She lets out a snorting sound from her nose and it's like she's sat beside me. She glides through the icy water towards the shore, she's in line with me and the Pine tree as she lands much closer to me than expected. Luckily, I'm almost as white as my surroundings and blend in quite well. Thick powdery flakes continue to fall, and one is spiralling down gently and lands on her nose as she lifts her head up to taste the air. A few flakes have congregated on her head and back and she shakes them off upwards from where they came. She's only about thirty feet away and she's showing signs of having a cub or two in a natal holt nearby as I can just make out a teat as she rolls on the frozen shore. Slipping back into the water she begins to fish again, coming up with small fish and the occasional Shore Crab. I'm not sure if I can feel my hands or my face and I really don't care, as this is a truly wonderful moment, surrounded by the imposing white. The Otter clambers up onto the shore, less than twenty feet away and begins to roll again on the snowy blanket, arching her body all the way around and chasing her own tail, snowflakes are flying everywhere, and she seems to be enjoying it like it's a game. She rolls again and again in front of me. I wonder what she'd make of me if she suddenly looked up and saw me gazing at her - looks like she's having too much fun to care as she slides effortlessly around and around on the icy shore. I can't take my eyes off her as she slumps down for a brief rest. The snowfall has come to an abrupt end, signalling her time to slip back into the water, drifting with purpose in and out of the mini icebergs scattered over the bay. She startles a male Eider who tries to take flight, feet scrambling against the water as fast as he can and flapping his wings ferociously. Finally, he's airborne and away, winging his way over the bay and giving a second low flyby. The

Otter, meanwhile, has drifted away and is heading in front of a snow-covered backdrop and onto the land next to the old forest. She sits prominently for a few minutes then rolls over in a drift of snow to rid herself of some of the salty water. She clambers through the White Heather and disappears through the wall of tall Pine trees and then she's gone, hopefully to join her cubs in a warm and cosy holt, away from a harsh, but beautiful winter.

The High Tide Otter

The Otter sits motionless on the exposed fossilised tree roots as the tide falls around him, he barely twitches as the large drops of rain pound the top of his head which is now flattened by the persistent downpour.

The large black rock encrusted with Limpets that's dressed in dark seaweed that I'm wedged against is holding my cover for now. He's sure there's something there to be checked out, although his vision isn't the best, his hearing, and especially, his sense of smell is impeccable. His nose is the only thing that's moving as it constantly smells the air as he continues to stare in my direction. The heavy drops fall slowly down my face as I resist the temptation to make any movement and wipe the water from my eyes. He's testing to see what I am and if I'm a threat to him. He knows he has the safety of water between us and he'll use it if he feels the need to. After five minutes he relaxes his back and drapes his flat rudder of a tail beside his back legs as he eases himself lower onto the flattest part of the wood, he looks at peace and I feel accepted by him. It's taken more than three months of watching him almost every day for him to react to me like this.

The tide has almost completely retreated as the lone male wades through the remaining still water and squelches up onto a clump of fiery yellow seaweed, a fair bit closer to me and where I'm sat. He's not as alert as he was and spends barely any time sniffing the air or looking around before laying his head down on the bed of comfy seaweed. His nose is pointed upwards and his oversized whiskers droop at the ends as the rain carries on falling, his blinks are getting longer and it's not long before almost all his head is immersed on his coastal pillow. The shallow flickering of his eyes is getting deeper and, finally, he blinks for one last time as his eyes close. His front spayed webbed feet and head are the only visible features against the seaweed as I wipe my face and adjust my feet to settle down for the duration of his nap. There's no sign on the horizon of the relentless rain relinquishing but the cold wind left over from the winter has passed and a hint of spring fills the air.

His coat is drenched but the fresh rain is washing off the salt from the sea as he sleeps; he's not at all phased by it and looks in a deep sleep as he fidgets like he's having a dream and moves his paw to cover his broad grainy nose. I detach myself from the black rock and skulk to a slightly more sheltered position at the base of a small crag with an overhanging Rowan tree. I'm a little bit closer and I can see his nostrils flare heavily as he breathes in and out.

A dainty Redshank ambles within a foot of the Otter and is completely unaware of him until he plucks an insect within inches of his head and looks briefly startled before continuing to forage on the low tide. The Otter was unaware too and didn't move a muscle. The rain hitting the rocks around me makes a shallow drumming sound like an opening to a traditional Celtic folk song and the lighter wind coming in from the sea provides the mellow noise like a stringed instrument as I hum random words in my head to fit the tune. After a few more minutes of make-believe music, it's almost complete stillness again from both the Otter and the tide until his nose twitches and his eyes stir. He reminds me of watching Squeaks sleeping in her makeshift holt with her head poking out. The Otter opens-up his eyes briefly and slowly raises his head to look left, then right, then straight at me, he's aware of my presence but just seeps back into the salty weeds and drifts away again as the rain softens slightly.

Light is starting to break through the blanket of cold coloured clouds and is flickering a handful of shards onto the hillside and filtering down onto the sea. It's been eight long minutes watching the changing of the scape as the rain falls with less and less force and the Otter remains like a cosy statue wedged in the seaweed as the light and colours around him change. A small flock of Gannets gather high up in the middle of the Sound as a few late departing Geese bark out as they head north, past the sloping hillside. Nothing seems to disturb the Otter until a Gull in a random panic squawks loudly upwards, aimed at the sky, and the Otter's eyes open with intensity as he looks at the nearby Gull with an unimpressed glare. The Gull continues to call loudly upwards towards the murky, dark clouds as the culprit for the noise appears and glides effortlessly in a circular way; it's a juvenile Sea Eagle spreading his wings to signal the stopping of the rain, much to the disgust of the Gull who's now taken flight to try and harass the young Eagle up in the sky. The Eagle is almost across the Sound before the Gull has even got any decent height to be a problem for the Eagle and drops back down and onto the top of a Pine tree near the point as the Eagle heads further away and out of sight behind the distant hills. The Otter still has his eyes wide open and looks grumpily in my direction before snorting with tiredness towards the empty rock where the Gull shouted, he's anything but impressed as he grooms his lower back and nibbles gently at his tail which is changing from dark to light brown as it slowly dries. The sound of popping seaweed is overtaken by the gnawing sound from the Otter as a Raven interrupts and gives a full-throated croak from high up in the nearby wood, followed by an almost laughing call from an unseen Jay. For a moment, I'm sure both our plans are to blend completely into the landscape and go unseen from everything, he's more inconspicuous than me sitting under the Rowan, even if I am well-tucked to the crag. If I was an Otter, I think I'd be most like him. Squeaks was generally ecstatic most of the time, but he's much more of a loner, snorting, grunting and generally showing his displeasure at things. He wants to go unseen, but he has a role to do in this territory and when he's not sleeping it's almost impossible to see him still. Of all the Otters I've watched, he's the one that reminds me the most of Squeaks, even though he's much larger, and male, and shares hardly any of her traits. It's the way he stares at me sometimes, it makes me feel the way she did; it's not sadness or longing and the word to describe it escapes me. Maybe it's because he's the Otter I've spent most time with since her. The male's finished his preening ritual and looks hungry again and slides into the water which isn't even deep enough to cover his whole back as the tide's a long way out, twists and turns through the exposed seaweed and brings out the brightest green Shore Crab I've ever seen. He thrashes it against the rock being careful not to have another encounter with its pincers. He's disarmed the crab with ease and the crunching sound carries some distance to where I'm sat, but not for long, as he falls back into the shallow water leaving the discarded pieces of the crustacean upon the rock for the Gulls and the Hooded Crows to scavenge upon. It's not long before they arrive and fight amongst themselves for the Otter's leftovers. The Crow clearly wins the race by swooping in low, snatching the crab remains and flying hastily towards the woods, leaving the two Gulls to scream at each other and stare down at the empty rock. The Otter carries on foraging and he's found a deeper pool that he can submerge in, kicks up sand from the bottom which turns the pool into a churned-up caramel brown colour, the water swirling around and around like a low pressured jacuzzi. Whatever he's chasing must be big, or he's just having a bit of fun. His head pops up with a glum expression upon his face, the salty water falls off his back as he lands onto a strip of sand that looks oily reflective as more and more light filters through the ever-increasing cracks in the sky. As usual, a Robin gets the hint from the change in the weather as he performs his song from above me in the Rowan to anyone who'll listen. The sweet little song sounds like a message being cast out to sea where the dog Otter is currently busily sifting through, and underneath the forest of the seaweed in the shallows. The sun shows itself for the first time today and is already tilting downwards toward the end of the day. Half of the sky is still dominated by cloud, but the other half has more bright, wintry blue than dark and with the wind becoming almost non-existent it looks like a battle in the sky which could still go either way. The foraging Otter has had enough and heads at speed back to the fiery mound of seaweed, clambers through it like he's looking for the exact spot he slept in earlier, and after moving a few strands, he seems to find the spot and settles down in it once more.

The sun which has only just shown itself for the first time, is sliding away just above the hills. There's a rumbling sound from the sea as the tide begins to turn, it sounds a little bit like mild watery thunder as the first set of small waves lap against the tiny spit of sand moving a scattering of broken shells up the beach and dragging them back into the sea. The Otter seems to have been triggered by the change and stands up like he's proud of himself. Despite the halting of the rain, lingering drops from the Rowan above me still fall on my head. The Otter rolls over onto his back and paws away at his belly like he's tickling himself; his stomach is dry and a light caramel colour and the rest of his body changes quickly to light brown as it dries from the lingering light. A Heron lazily flies up the coast on stiffened wings before landing a little too closely to the Otter, stopping his casual grooming and pointing his nose towards the large water bird, he looks agitated that anything has dared to come within his area. The Heron pays the Otter no attention at all and just aims his large bill at the shallows below him; he strides in slow-motion, in the rising low water, as the Otter intently watches on. The Heron stops mid-flow, arches back its neck and freezes, stays statuesque for half a minute, then, in one fluid motion, he strikes snakelike into the water, pulls back his head and reveals a small fish within his beak. The Otter refuses to watch on any longer and charges at full bounding speed towards the Heron who rapidly unfolds his slate grey wings and pushes away as quickly as his heavy frame will allow. The Otter gets within feet of the Heron just in time to watch it wheel away and drift around the coast. That weirdly brought me back to watching Squeaks chasing the butterfly out of her enclosure, that curiosity and stubbornness to share their space got the better of them both.

The Otter remains half-submerged in an ever-rising tide. The sun behind the sea and the hills has fallen out of sight as the cloud that covered half the sky fades fast. It doesn't feel like time has passed by that quickly, but the water level has covered the sand and the smaller rocks in the bay. A handful of Seals bob up in the water a little way off, they look to be just hanging there as if waiting to be fed. I'm sure the high tide will bring plenty of fish from deeper waters. The Otter paddles further out to the only cluster of rocks that hasn't been taken by the tide, he scrapes up the side and deposits a spraint onto the flattest rock; he doesn't stay there long and swiftly makes his way into the water. He dives deeply under a floating mass of seaweed that's risen-up, the water swirls and sways as he swims underneath trying to dislodge any larger prey that's hiding in the cover. He emerges up through the seaweed, I can just see his eyes peering back towards the shoreline; he drops his head under the water and moves away towards the edges. The spot the Otter slept on is now completely engulfed by the high tide as the Otter floats past.

The light is changing at the rate of the tide as the Otter turns into a half-silhouetted state, he carries on gliding out of the bay. I tentatively move from under the umbrella of the Rowan for the first time in what feels like an eternity, scurrying up the side of the black crag to get a bit of height. I can see the Otter better from here. He heads in the direction of the rocky outcrop that splits the bays in half and veers towards the rocky beach ahead of him. He always lines himself up with the small stream that runs down from the wood, stares at the shore to briefly check for signs of danger, and when he's ready, and in his own time, he makes his way out of the water, getting the all clear and skulks out of the high tide and up onto the black pebbly beach. I watch him disappear onto the darkening shoreline and away up the base of the stream, he's kept me company and amused me for the last few hours, but now as darkness descends on the coastline an invisible blanket of cold has arrived - it's time for me to leave too.

Epilogue

After Ten Years

It's been ten years to the day since my first encounter with a wild Otter. I'm on the Island close to where I saw him, roughly at this time of day. The large sea loch and surrounding hills still look like I have half of the world in front of me; the sun's risen and fallen a thousand times since then and still looks beautiful as it sits waiting to fall above the wooded hillside.

The water is relatively still as the tide leaves the flat, rocky shoreline I'm perched on, littered with pools of water left behind by the tide. I can see my watery reflection in the nearest pool and how much I've changed since my first visit here. The sky above me looks moody as it writes its own story on the distant hills and sea below.

The journey's been an awakening; I've exhausted all corners in my pursuit of the wild Otter. It's been an adventure like nothing else I've been through or will go through again. I still can't believe I'm here, it's almost too hard to visualise being mentally trapped in my room, locked inside my head and afraid to go out outside – yet, here I am, with a huge slice of the world in front of me. My thoughts of past journeys and distant traumas are interrupted by the slightest ripple behind an exposed rock that's touched by swaying seaweed. I wait like I always do for more movement in the water. Then, coming from behind the rock,

an Otter...

He's low down in the water as he glides through like a shallow wave being pushed against the soft outgoing tide. The Otter wanders across the water towards a low-lying dark rock, skulks up out of the water and reveals his full body shape from his broad nose to the tip of his tail. He shakes the water off his fur and stands proudly upon the rock for a few seconds. I wonder if he's a relative of my first Otter all those years ago. He doesn't hang about for long as he slips away into the shallowing water. The light around me falls as the sun gets ushered away by the clouds. A drop of the shoulder, an arch of the body, followed instantly by a flick of the tail and he's submerged into another world under the surface. I sit and watch the water return to calm around the place he dived. He emerges a little further out, near where the two hills slope down and almost meet near the mouth of the sea. I sit and watch as the silhouetted shape of the Otter drifts across the opening of the sea loch and away. He's gone for now, but it won't be the last Otter I'll ever see.

Without a chance meeting with that wonderful little Otter called, Squeaks, none of this would've been at all possible.

Printed in Great Britain
by Amazon

62263291R00130